FINLAND

BY LINDA HUTCHISON

LUCENT
BOOKS®

THOMSON

————★————™

GALE

San Diego • Detroit • New York • San Francisco • Cleveland • New Haven, Conn. • Waterville, Maine • London • Munich

I would like to thank my sons, Raul and Erik Rathmann, for their
continued support; my editors, Viqi Wagner and Jennifer Skancke,
for their abilities to help me better organize and present this
information; and Eija Herrala Blocker and Vincent Blocker for
generously offering many valuable insights and clarifications.

LIBRARY OF CONGRESS CATALOGING-IN-PUBLICATION DATA

Linda, Hutchison.
  Finland / by Linda Hutchison.
    p. cm. — (Modern nations of the world)
Contents: At the top of the world—From nomads and vikings to kings and czars—From
farm and forest to urban high tech—High ideals on solid ground—Never far from the
forest—Celebrating nature in arts and entertainment—Maintaining balance in the
twenty-first century.
  Includes bibliographical references and index.
  ISBN 1-59018-518-8 (alk. paper)
I. Title. II. Modern nations of the world (San Diego, Calif.)

Printed in the United States of America

CONTENTS

INTRODUCTION

FROM THE REMOTE EDGE TO CUTTING EDGE

In the last twenty years, Finland has emerged from its remote location on the top edge of the world to become a leader in cutting-edge technology. As home to number-one cell phone maker Nokia, Finland has introduced its technology to the world and embraced it enthusiastically at home—from students and workers in the cities to reindeer herders in the far north.

This emergence from a remote and little-known nation might seem unusual, but Finland has always been unique. Although it is a part of Europe, it lies apart from its neighbors, both geographically and culturally. It is considered a Nordic country—meaning "northern"—but its language and history are different from that of the other Nordic countries. It is also considered by some to be Scandinavian, bordering Norway and Sweden and near Denmark. Others call it a Baltic country, grouping it with Russia and other nations around the Baltic Sea, like Germany, Estonia, Latvia, and Lithuania. The truth is that Finland is a little bit of all of these—Nordic, Scandinavian, Baltic, and European—and yet it is its own country, too.

More than anything, Finland has been defined by its forests. Covering 70 percent of the land, they have provided resources and refuge for hardy hunters, explorers, and farmers for thousands of years. Eventually the forests also became a source of myths and an integral, intertwined part of Finnish personal and national identity. These myths, songs, poems, and stories were ambitiously collected by a Finnish country doctor, Dr. Elias Lönnrot, in the 1800s. He named them *The Kalevala: Or Poems of the Kaleva District*.

Dominating *The Kalevala* are three main characters—the Big Three—Väinämöinen, Ilmarinen, and Lemminkäinen. Väinämöinen is the chief of the three, the eternal sage, old and wise, inventor of the kantele. Ilmarinen is the forger of metals, the craftsman, the steady, competent worker. Lemminkäinen is the lover, the restless one with a roving eye and mind. In some ways, these characters have represented Finland itself, and still do, one hundred and fifty years later.

Like Väinämöinen, the Finns acknowledge their ancient past and have built a modern nation on the wisdom of ageless principles. Like Ilmarinen, they are dependable workers and builders. Finally, like Lemminkäinen, they are individualistic lovers of life who look to the future. A combination of all three, Finns respect the past, work in the present, and allow for future innovation. To them, Finland, like Kaleva, is a unique, magical land—and yet very real.

1

AT THE TOP OF THE WORLD

Finland sits on top of Europe, just 1,370 miles from the North Pole. Its capital city, Helsinki, is the northernmost capital on the European continent. Because of this location, Finland has evolved into one of the most ruggedly beautiful countries in the world.

Carved out by retreating glaciers, its valleys and bays filled with water, creating thousands of lakes, coastal fjords, and islands. Dense forests grew over much of this cold land where only the hardiest of humans chose to live. Those who did learned to live in harmony with the land, which has shaped their history, culture, and economy.

LOCATION, BOUNDARIES, AND SIZE

Finland is located in the northeast corner of Europe. One-third of the country lies above the Arctic Circle. It shares borders with Norway on the north (451 miles), Sweden on the west (353 miles), and Russia on the east (788 miles). It is also bordered by two arms of the Baltic Sea: the Gulf of Bothnia on the west and the Gulf of Finland on the south.

Finland occupies approximately 130,000 square miles: more than the state of New Mexico, but less than Montana or California. Its shape has been compared to that of a woman holding up her right arm.

Compared to Norway and Sweden, Finland is relatively flat, with rolling hills and sandy and rocky ridges. Its highest point is Mt. Haltia, just 4,355 feet above sea level, in the northwest part of the country. Since the glaciers melted, the land has been rising, about one-fifth of an inch every year.

Approximately 70 percent of Finland is covered with forest. Lakes cover another 10 percent. In fact, Finland has more lakes than any other country in the world: 187,888.

COASTAL LOWLANDS

Finland has three distinct geographical regions: the coastal lowlands, the interior plateau, and the northern uplands. A coastal plain from twenty to eighty miles wide fringes the seven hundred miles of Finland's west and south coasts. It consists of gently rolling hills, rocky ridges, peninsulas, bays, and thousands of islands.

The climate here is slightly warmer than in the rest of the country, warmed by the Baltic Sea and winds from the Gulf

Stream off Norway. The coldest months are December, January, and February, when temperatures range from 14 to 32°F. Winter lasts about one hundred days, with snow on the ground from November to March. The warmest months are July and August, when temperatures average about 65 to 70°F. The annual rainfall is about nineteen inches a year, with most storms occurring in the fall and winter.

The south coast is the most urbanized part of Finland, with many natural harbors. One of these shelters is Helsinki, Finland's largest and capital city. In the eastern part of this area, the influence of Russia is still visible, from old forts to pollution from pulp factories.

The west coast, on the other hand, has been influenced by its proximity to Sweden. Some of Finland's oldest towns and cities were founded here by the Swedes as trading centers and farming areas. Today there are many medieval stone churches and castles left over from seven hundred years of Swedish rule. One area of the west coast is called the Swedish Coast or Par-

Its topography carved out by retreating glaciers, Finland is relatively flat and features nearly 200,000 lakes like this one in Savonlinna in the south.

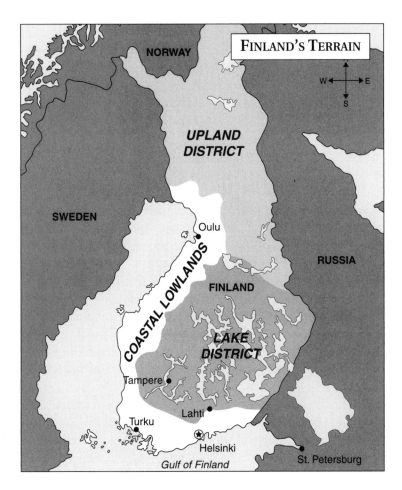

allel Sweden because it includes so many Swedish-speaking people. The western coastal plain is flatter and drier than the south. It includes farms; some lakes and marshes; dense forests; well-preserved, quaint seaside villages; and some of Finland's most isolated beaches and islands.

Finland has about 179,500 islands, and 95,000 of these are located off the south and west coasts. These coastal islands vary from barren, rocky islets to large archipelagos (groups of islands) with dense forests, wildflowers, and harbors. Many are linked to the coastline and to each other with bridges, tunnels, or ferries. Some are inhabited, and many others are home to historical landmarks, amusement parks, museums, campgrounds, bike paths, and fishing areas. One of the southernmost islands—Bengtsskär, fifteen miles off the southwest coast—has the tallest lighthouse in Scandinavia.

INTERIOR PLATEAU

Finland's interior plateau is a vast area of interconnected lakes, short rivers, canals, rapids, islands, and beaches in south-central Finland. Most of Finland's lakes are located in this area, which is about sixty miles wide. About three hundred to six hundred feet above sea level, much of the area is forested. The climate in the interior is similar to that of the coast, although there can be more thunderstorms and heat waves in the summer. (To the Finns, anything above 77°F is considered hot.)

At the very center of the interior is the Lake District, or Lakeland (Saimaa), a popular vacation area in summer and winter. Many Finns own or rent cottages and come here in the summer for boating and fishing, and in the winter for skiing and ice fishing. The local people—Savolaiset (people of Savo)—have their own dialect and are known for their easygoing attitude toward life. Steamboats churn through many of the lakes. Once the main form of transportation for Lakelanders, they are now used to carry tourists. In the Kolovesi National Park, visitors can rent long rowboats. Motorboats are not allowed, so as not to disturb the rare Saimaa seals.

The eastern part of the interior plateau is known as North Karelia (*Karjala* in Finnish). Still a less-populated area, it has been a trading outpost for centuries and is one of the few areas in the country where a brown bear can be spotted. It was originally a mining area. Except for its forests, Finland has few natural resources. In Karelia, some minerals were discovered, such as copper, iron, zinc, gold, and silver, and building materials such as red granite, graphite, limestone, and quartz. A multihued mineral called spectrolite is mined here and is very popular in Finnish jewelry making.

Karelia has been influenced in many ways—from architecture to food—by Russian culture on the other side of the border. Throughout the centuries, the border itself has shifted as Sweden, Russia, and Finland claimed the land. In the nineteenth century, the area inspired many romantic-era artists and musicians who saw its forests and disputed land as a symbol of Finland and a separate Finnish identity.

In the south part of Karelia, only a narrow strip of land still belongs to Finland. In 1856, a canal was built in this area from the town of Lappeenranta on Lake Saimaa to Vyborg (*Viipuri* in

LUMINOUS NIGHTS

There are many who roam about in the northern summer night,
especially as Sunday dawns. The reasons are many, but the
outward condition is the same for all, the same today as in times
gone by: the night's luminosity.
—F.E. Sillanpää, People in the Summer Night

At the top of the world, the nighttime sky takes on new, luminous meanings, as Nobel Prize–winning author F.E. Sillanpää wrote seventy years ago. In the spring and summer, from about May 17 to July 27, there is constant daylight in the far north. At its lowest point, the midnight sun, as it is called, hovers over the horizon. Farther south, daylight lasts for about nineteen hours, the sun rising about 4:00 A.M. and setting about 11:00 P.M. Even after it sets, it does not get completely dark and people are often outdoors making up for time lost in the winter. As late as midnight, many are walking, jogging, cycling, swimming, boating, or fishing.

Conversely, the sun does not come up at all for about fifty days in the winter because the earth is tilting away from the sun, just as it does not go down for seventy days in the summer because the earth is tilting toward it. Although these extremes affect only the northernmost part of Lapland, the long nights and days stretch over most of Finland.

North of Rovaniemi, the capital of Lapland, there is no daylight at all between about November 25 and January 15. There is only an eerie twilight, which the Finns call "blue time." In Rovaniemi, the sun rises for about two hours a day during this period. In the central and southern parts of Finland, the sun comes out for about six hours in the winter, rising about 9:30 in the morning and setting about 3:00 in the afternoon.

Another form of light also occurs at the top of the world. Called the "northern lights," or aurora borealis, these swirling streamers of greenish white light appear to dance through the sky, turning red, blue, and violet at their lower edges. Although they are visible year-round, they are most striking in the darker skies of winter. This light show has captivated people for centuries. The Greeks called them "blood rain." The Romans named them after Aurora, the goddess of the dawn.

According to an ancient Laplander legend, they are caused by a giant fox swishing its tail above the frozen tundra. (The Finnish word for northern lights—*revontulet*—means "fires of the fox.") In reality, they are caused by protons, or energy particles, from the sun colliding with the earth's magnetic field, which pulls them toward the North and South Poles. At the South Pole, they are called southern lights, or aurora australis (southern dawn).

Finnish) on the Gulf of Finland forty-three miles to the south. Today Lappeenranta is Finland's largest inland port and Lake Saimaa attracts many Russian tourists. Vyborg is part of Russia, but the Finns retain the right to use the canal.

NORTHERN UPLANDS

The top third of Finland comprises the northern uplands and includes the provinces of Oulu and Lapland (*Lappi* in Finnish). Here the climate is the coldest. Temperatures average about 55 to 65°F in the summer and 0 to 14°F in the winter. Winter can last up to two hundred days, from October to May. About twenty-three inches of rain falls each year, half as snow.

The province of Oulu—between the Lake District and Lapland—is Finland's most rugged area. It includes more dense forest, more isolated lakes and rivers, and more animal and plant life than other parts of the country. The far eastern part is accessible only with a tour guide. There are more hilly areas in the far north, close to Sweden and Norway, but fewer trees. The dense forests of Oulu gradually thin out into forests of smaller birch trees and then into the tundra of the far north. Tundra is a mucky topsoil with a frozen subsoil.

The western part, on the Gulf of Bothnia, has become more urbanized. Before highways were built in the twentieth century, many of the rivers were used for transporting lumber and tar (used for shipbuilding) to the port towns on the gulf. Now parts of Oulu are being developed and used for summer and winter resorts.

Lapland is Finland's coldest and least-populated province, with about two hundred thousand residents. About sixty-five hundred of these are Saami, descendents of early inhabitants who herded reindeer and lived in tepeelike structures called *kota.* Today the reindeer are semidomesticated. They wander freely across huge cooperatives where fences run for miles. The Saami, who now live in houses, round up the reindeer twice a year using snowmobiles and helicopters and communicating with cell phones. Most of the residents of Lapland live in the southern part of the province.

Lapland includes the oldest and largest national parks in Finland. These have become popular destinations for hikers, mountain bikers, river rafters, fishing enthusiasts, and skiers. The west part of Lapland, called Sea Lapland, on the Gulf of

Bothnia, has become a prosperous area, attracting new high-tech businesses around the University of Oulu.

Rivers

Finland's two longest rivers are located in Lapland. The Kemijoki flows from the central part of Lapland 345 miles southwest to Kemi, on the Gulf of Bothnia (*joki* means "river" in Finnish). Most of Finland's northern rivers drain into the Kemijoki. Dominated by paper and pulp mills, the river was used until the early nineteen nineties to float lumber down to Kemi, a major export harbor. Now a road parallels the river and is used for transporting the lumber.

The Torniojoki begins in northern Sweden and flows 320 miles southwest to Tornio on the Gulf of Bothnia, just 9 miles north of Kemi. It marks Finland's western border with Sweden. In medieval times, this river valley was a popular trading area and was used by the Swedes to set up tax-collecting offices. Today a road parallels the river and is the main route up into north-coast fjords of Norway.

The Torniojoki includes the longest free-flowing rapids in Finland, and is popular in summer for river rafting and fishing for salmon and whitefish. The whitefish are caught with special long-handled nets and cooked out in the open. Many rafts include cooking stoves and saunas (steam baths in which steam is provided by water thrown on hot stones).

Flora and Fauna

Most of Finland's plant life and wildlife are found throughout the country, with the exception of Lapland and the cities. Even in the cities, however, the forests are not far away, since they cover 70 percent of the country. Of this, 45 percent are evergreen pine, which grow mostly on dry ground and sand ridges; 37 percent are evergreen spruce, which grow in dense and dark forests with little undergrowth; and 15 percent are deciduous birch, which drop their leaves in winter. The remaining 3 percent includes lindens, elms, and ashes, which grow only in southwest Finland.

Since so much of Finland is covered with lakes and marshes, many plants are those that thrive near water, such as mosses and lichens. In all, there are 1,227 varieties of plants and shrubs, 800 of moss, and 1,000 of lichen.

Finland also includes 67 species of mammals, 370 species of birds, and 77 species of fish. The largest and rarest mammal in Finland is the brown bear. Others include the moose, fox, lynx, and wolf. In Lapland there are about 230,000 semi-domesticated reindeer. Wild reindeer are rare. Other small animals include the lemming, hedgehog, muskrat, beaver, otter, and hare. Of the 370 bird species in Finland, many are waterbirds, including swans and 60 percent of the world's population of goldeneye and billed sandpipers. Forest birds include the willow warbler, woodpecker, raven, and owl, and in Lapland the silver jay, which sometimes follow people. Sparrows are common in the cities and towns. Finland's cold inland waters include salmon and rapu (a freshwater crustacean). Herring are plentiful in the Baltic Sea. The only poisonous snake is the viper, whose bite will not kill a healthy person. In June and July, large mosquitoes can be very annoying to people.

Finland is home to a wide variety of animal species. Of the country's sixty-seven mammal species, the brown bear is the largest and most rare.

REINDEER

The reindeer is a member of the deer family that wanders in a large area covering the top fourth of the world. Most of this arctic and subarctic area, which ranges from Europe and Asia to North America, is remote and, until recent times, little populated except by reindeer herders. The earliest evidence of reindeer herding dates to about 30,000 B.C. in the Yukon area of Canada, where remains of corrals used to round up the animals have been found. (In Canada and Alaska, reindeer are called caribou.)

In Finland, a rock carving dating to about 3000 B.C. has been found that depicts a herding enclosure used by the Saami to catch reindeer and elk. When the Saami began to herd and domesticate reindeer rather than just hunt them, they developed a close relationship with the animals and used them for many things. They were used (and still are) for transportation (as pack animals and to pull sleds) and for milk. Butchered, their meat and intestines were used for eating and their skin for tents, clothing, and shoes. Even the tendons and sinews were used for sewing.

The reindeer is the only deer where both the male and the female have antlers. The male uses his for fighting and the female for protecting her young. The antlers are shed and regrown each year. Reindeer hooves are wide and rounded and concave, which allows them to walk on icy ground and to dig in snow or swamps. Their thick fur, which is light brown in summer and whiter in winter, keeps them warm and even helps them float in water. They are strong animals. A typical male of 250 pounds can pull up to twice his weight on a sled and travel forty miles a day. In the wild, reindeer live about ten years. They spend most of the day eating lichens and moss in the winter and leaves in the summer.

Reindeer used to travel hundreds of miles between winter and summer grazing grounds in herds of up to two hundred thousand animals. Today they live in privately owned herding districts. Each reindeer is marked with cuts in the ears. Twice a year, the herders (mostly Saami in Finland) round them up, selecting them for further breeding or for slaughtering. A hundred years ago, most Saami lived in tents and used sleds to herd reindeer. Today most live in houses or mobile homes and use cell phones, snowmobiles, and even helicopters in their roundups.

HELSINKI

Helsinki is the capital city of Finland and its largest city, with about 525,000 people. Located on the south coast of Finland, it is called the White Daughter of the Baltic because its light-colored buildings are visible from far out at sea. According to historian Fred Singleton, Helsinki was known for its beautiful buildings even before it was completely built: "As early as 1830, 40 years before completion, a foreign visitor wrote that the Finns were 'converting a heap of rocks into a beautiful city.'" [1]

Helsinki is a compact city of about 426 square miles, built on a rocky peninsula. Despite its small size, it has an open feel with slivers of forest and sea extending inside the city. According to Singleton:

> The center of Helsinki is built on a peninsula, pene-trated by arms of the sea which provide excellent an-chorages for ships. . . . Despite the congestion of a restricted site, the central area has a spacious air. There are several wide boulevards and open squares and some of the earliest municipal parks in northern Eu-rope. [2]

The center of the city includes its main harbor, an open market called the Fish Market, the Senate Square with gov-ernment buildings and a university, and Esplanade Park with many shops, restaurants, and outdoor cafés. Helsinki's archi-tecture is a unique combination of European, Russian, and Scandinavian. Currently there are no buildings over twelve stories high in Helsinki, but plans are underway to build the city's first high-rise (twenty-six stories) in 2004.

The yellow and blue stone buildings in the Senate Square were designed in the early 1800s by a German architect, C.L. Engel (1778–1840), who lived in St. Petersburg, Russia, just 236 miles to the east. The style he used, called neoclassical or Empire, was popular in Russia at the time. The square, which also includes a statue of Russian czar Alexander II, is often used as a backdrop for movies set in Russia, such as *Gorky Park* and *Dr. Zhivago*.

Even though parts of Helsinki have a Russian and Euro-pean flavor, it is very much a modern, sophisticated city with more than seven hundred restaurants, several museums and parks, a zoo, and the University of Helsinki. In the summer, Helsinki residents take advantage of the long summer nights and are often outdoors until 10:00 or 11:00 P.M., sitting in out-door cafés or walking, jogging, cycling, fishing, and playing other sports. Offshore, more than three hundred islands are connected to the city with bridges, water taxis, and ferries. In the cold winter months, when the waters freeze, people ski and walk across the ice. Regular ferries connect Helsinki with Stockholm, Sweden, just 160 miles west across the Gulf of Bothnia, and with Tallinn, Estonia, 50 miles south across the Gulf of Finland.

OTHER CITIES

Two other large cities in Finland are actually suburbs of Helsinki. In all, more than a million people, or a fifth of Finland's population, live in the greater Helsinki area. Espoo, the second-largest city, with about 200,000 people, is just ten miles west of Helsinki. It includes the planned community of Tapiola Garden City, designed as a model combination of apartments and houses carefully interspersed with stores, schools, and parks. Another suburban city, Vantaa, the fourth largest, with a population of 178,000, is located nine miles north of Helsinki and is the site of the airport and an aviation museum.

TWO SPECIAL PROVINCES: LAPLAND AND ALAND

Two of Finland's six provinces—Lapland and Aland—extend beyond a strict definition of borders. Although they are officially considered part of Finland, they are not completely.

In the north, the province of Lapland (*Lappi* in Finnish) covers almost the whole top half of Finland. The least-populated province, it is home to about two hundred thousand people, including four thousand native Saami.

The territory of Lapland spreads across a much wider area, including northern Norway, Sweden, and Russia. In Norway, the area is called Finnmark. It is Norway's largest county and has the largest population of Saami: about forty thousand out of its total population of seventy-five thousand people. In Sweden, the area is called Lappland, and about seventeen thousand Saami live there.

The other Finnish province that defies strict definition is Aland. Located midway between Finland and Sweden in the Gulf of Bothnia, it is a semiautonomous province with its own parliament, stamp, and flag. Most of its twenty-five thousand residents are Swedish speaking, yet they have developed their own distinct culture, not fully Swedish and not fully Finnish. They pay no taxes, and because they are in a demilitarized zone, they do not have to serve in the military.

Aland (meaning "river land") has been popular since Viking times as a trade center. It is actually Finland's largest archipelago, with more than sixty-four hundred islands. (Aland is the name of the main island and also the name of the province, which includes all the islands.) Many of the islands are linked to each other by bridges and ferries, making it a popular area for bicyclists. Finland's oldest historical landmarks are located on Aland, including medieval stone churches and castles. The capital city of Mariehamn attracts thousands of vacationers and tourists every summer. Named after the wife of a Russian czar, Mariehamn has two harbors and is known as "the town of a thousand linden trees."

Finland's third-largest city—Tampere—is located on a strip of land between two lakes in the Lake District, about 108 miles northwest of Helsinki. It has about 195,000 residents and more than two hundred small lakes. Originally founded as an industrial city (and sometimes called "the Manchester of Finland"), it has transformed itself into a cultural center and one of Finland's most visited areas. It offers lake cruises, a large amusement park, several film and music festivals, several museums, two universities, a research institute, a teaching hospital, and twelve professional theater companies. Most of its industries—including textiles, wood and paper products, machinery, and shoes—have moved to the outskirts of the city.

Turku is Finland's fifth-largest city, with 172,500 people. Located on the southwest coast of Finland, about 103 miles west of Helsinki, it is also Finland's oldest city, dating back to the 1200s. It was the original capital under Swedish rule. Its castle from 1280 is the country's most popular tourist attraction. It also has a university and more museums than Helsinki. Even though the capital was moved from Turku to Helsinki almost two hundred years ago, locals still refer to Helsinki as the "village to the east."

Inari Lake is one of the many lakes located in the northern province of Lapland, a region of Finland with only 200,000 residents.

Two other less-populated but busy cities are Oulu, with 120,000 residents, on the northwest corner of the Gulf of Bothnia, and Rovaniemi, with 35,000 residents, in Lapland. Oulu is a university town built on several islands. Its School of Technology has attracted many students, graduates, and new businesses. It has the country's oldest and biggest science museum and many outdoor cafés, as described by Lonely Planet travel-guide writers Jennifer Brewer and Markus Lehtipuu:

> Oulu—perhaps more than any other city in Finland—is a place where people insist on drinking their cold beer outside, in the sun, as soon as the snow melts. Wall-to-wall beer terraces flourish in summer . . . where you are serenaded by street musicians. [3]

Rovaniemi is the main city in Lapland, about 522 miles north of Helsinki. Up until World War II, it was a remote trading outpost. It was destroyed by the Germans when they retreated at the end of the war. Well-known Finnish architect Alvar Aalto (1898–1976) was hired to redesign the city. Its streets radiate from the center in the shape of reindeer antlers. Now a bustling tourist hub, Rovaniemi attracts visitors year-round. Many use the city as a base for wilderness adventures such as hiking and rafting. Others come to enjoy its festivals, museums devoted to Saami and Arctic culture, wilderness parks where polar bears are protected, and the official Santa Claus village and post office and Santapark.

Whether in the far north of the Arctic Circle, the maze of interior lakes and forests, or the coastal plains and islands, Finland, more than any other European country, bears the imprint of the retreating Ice Age. Its forests and lakes make it unique. According to environmentalist Eeva-Liisa Hallanaro, the mixture of the two makes Finland even more exceptional:

> What gives Finnish scenery its own particular charm is the interplay between these two elements. Even the densest forests are interspersed with the countless lakes, ponds and rivers; while even the largest lakes are dotted with tree-covered islands and promontories. [4]

Into this unique land located at the top of the world would wander some of the world's most daring and hardy people. These would include nomadic reindeer hunters and fishermen from central Russia and, later, explorers and traders from Sweden and Europe.

2

FROM NOMADS AND VIKINGS TO KINGS AND CZARS

In spite of its remote location, Finland has attracted people for thousands of years. Perhaps because of this location, its first inhabitants were hardy nomads who trekked in from the east and south, followed by daring Vikings from the west who sailed around the coastline.

Rich in fish, animals, birds, and trees, Finland eventually attracted two powerful and competing neighbors: Sweden to the west and Russia to the east. These two empires took turns occupying Finland: Sweden for seven hundred years and Russia for one hundred. The Finns were never fully taken over by their rulers, however. They remained at heart strong-willed nomads and explorers able to brave harsh occupations and living conditions and still retain their own identity.

EARLY INHABITANTS

In the last ten years, archaeologists have discovered that humans lived in Finland one hundred thousand years ago, before the last Ice Age (70,000 to 10,000 B.C.). After the earth warmed, the ice melted, the glaciers retreated, and the northern land rose, allowing plants and animals and eventually humans to survive. According to the most recent archaeological evidence, nomadic tribes began arriving in Finland about 10,000 to 8000 B.C. They fished along the coastline and hunted migrating birds and animals such as elk, reindeer, bears, beavers, and seals. It is not known exactly where these people came from. Current evidence suggests they came from the east, from what is now central Russia.

During the following centuries (from 7000 to 1800 B.C.), these Stone Age people used tools and weapons made of stone, bone, and wood and carved animal heads on ships and sculptures. They also buried their dead painted with red ochre (iron oxide), indicating a religious rite and belief in the afterlife.

Gradually the forests of pine and spruce began growing and spreading throughout the country. Originally a freshwater lake, the Baltic Sea opened up to the North Sea. As a result of these changes, other tribes of people began arriving in Finland from the east and from the south in Europe. They introduced new forms of pottery and weapons, domesticated animals, and began cultivating crops.

During the Bronze Age (1800 to 500 B.C.), people were living in primitive houses built of dirt, reeds, and straw. Although most still relied on fishing and hunting, they also began to trade throughout the country and with Europe and Russia. With bronze from Russia, they made jewelry and built more sophisticated weapons.

This trade continued to increase from 500 B.C. to A.D. 500, during the period called the Iron Age. In exchange for wood and furs, the early Finns imported salt, weapons, and gold

OUT OF THE SWAMPS

Where did the name Finn or Finland come from? There are several theories about its origins. One theory is that Finland comes from the French *fin de lande,* meaning "end of the land," because of its remote location. Another theory is based on Finland's many lakes and swamps. In Roman times, the area was called Fennia, from the Latin *fen,* meaning "swamp." Today, a fen is defined as a lowland covered wholly or partly with water. Finland literally means "land of swamps or marshes." This same origin also applies in Finnish: A swamp is *suo,* and Finland is *Suomi.*

Various ancient tribes and areas within Finland also took their names from the earth. From the Baltic word *sama,* meaning "land," evolved *hame,* meaning "inhabitant of the interior." The Hämäläiset tribe lived in Häme in central Finland. Today, Häme is one of Finland's six provinces. Similarly, the words *same* and *sabme,* meaning "hunter," evolved into *saami.* The Saami were hunters of reindeer and possibly the earliest inhabitants of Finland. As other tribes moved into Finland, the Saami gradually retreated farther north into Lapland.

Early references to Finland describe two groups of Finns. The Roman historian Tacitus referred to the "poor Finns" in A.D. 98. Most likely, he was referring to the Saami in the north, who lived more primitively than their southern neighbors. By 871, King Alfred of England distinguished between the Finns of Finnmark in the far north and the Finns of the Baltic in the south. About the same time, the Vikings began calling the Finns Lapps, meaning "small piece of cloth," because they thought they were unimportant.

from Scandinavia and from Europe (as far away as Rome). By this time, farming was firmly established, people lived in wood cabins or block houses, and they organized into villages. At least four distinct groups of people began to emerge. The first inhabitants, known as Saami, had moved farther north. (By the seventeenth century, they would mostly live in Lapland and be known as Lapps.) The Karjalaiset lived in Karelia, in the east part of Finland next to Russia. The Hämäläiset lived in Häme, in central Finland, and the Suomalaiset lived in Suomi, in southwest Finland.

Despite being separated by large areas of rugged wilderness, these groups were often at war with each other and built primitive forts and stone ramparts on hills to protect themselves. Within their regions, however, they followed a common law under chieftains. The population began to grow and prosper as agriculture expanded, new tribes arrived from Europe, and trading routes opened up through Europe and the rivers of Russia to the Middle East.

VIKINGS

About A.D. 800, groups of fierce and daring warriors called Vikings began sailing from Norway, Sweden, and Denmark in search of new land. Their own countries were becoming crowded, and since only firstborn sons could inherit land, younger sons left to find land and riches elsewhere. Most were farmers or traders who were good at extracting iron from ore and making powerful weapons. These weapons gave them confidence. They also built light, fast ships with high prows called *drakkers*. With square sails and room for one hundred oarsmen, these ships moved quickly and could be pulled close to shore. This gave the Vikings the advantage of surprise in their attacks.

For more than two hundred years, these Northmen, as Europeans called them, terrorized Europe and the Middle East. The Danish and Norwegian Vikings sailed west and south, sometimes together and sometimes apart. The Danish reached Great Britain, France, and Spain, and the Norwegians reached Iceland, Greenland, and Newfoundland (eastern Canada), five hundred years before Columbus spotted America.

It was the Swedish Vikings who sailed east, across the Baltic and into Russia. They traded furs and amber for gold, silver, and luxury items. They built fortresses on the Aland Is-

In the ninth century, Swedish Vikings sailed to Finland's Aland Islands, where they established several fortresses.

lands and on the southwest coast of Finland. They built trading ports in Novgorod and Kiev in Ukraine. Although they took some Finnish men with them on their voyages and married Finnish women, the Vikings were pirates more than empire builders and never became a permanent power in Finland. Today, their influence can be seen mostly in the design of Finnish jewelry.

SWEDES

By the time the Vikings sailed their last voyage in the mid-eleventh century, the countries around Finland were struggling for power. Not strongly unified, Finland became a buffer zone between Sweden in the west and Russia in the east and, for a while, Denmark in the south. It was also caught in a parallel struggle between Roman Catholicism in the west and the Eastern Orthodox faith in the east. This struggle would dominate Finland for the next eight hundred years.

By the mid-twelfth century, Sweden had become a stronger nation than Finland. It was more unified and had closer contacts with Europe. Encouraged by an English pope, the Swedes began a series of military and religious crusades into Finland. Many Finns had already converted to Catholicism and were allied with Swedish settlers. The crusaders wanted to strengthen this alliance and convert the Finns who were not Catholic or who followed the Orthodox faith in the east.

Under Sweden's King Erik, the first crusade landed on Finland's shores in 1155. It was led by an English bishop, Henry of Uppsala, who was killed within a year. (There are conflicting accounts of his death. Some say he was killed by Finnish rebels, and others say he was killed by a peasant angry at Henry for having approached his wife when she was alone.) By the end of the following century, in 1296, Henry would be declared the patron saint of Turku and laid to rest in its cathedral, which had been made the seat of government and church headquarters.

Two more crusades followed, in 1238 and 1293, pushing farther north and east where the Swedish built fortified castles. To attract Swedish settlers to Finland, the Swedish government

THE FINNISH FLAG

Finland's national flag is a blue cross on a white background, representing its lakes and snow. It was first introduced in 1863, the same year Finnish was recognized as an official language of the country. Although Finland was still a part of Russia, the flag was adopted and hoisted on Finnish ships to keep them from being attacked by Russian enemies. It was officially adopted in 1918, a year after Finland became independent.

As in the United States, the flag can be flown throughout the year by both private individuals or business and government organizations. A few days in Finland are considered official flagging days, when all government organizations, offices, and schools are obligated to fly the flag. These include: February 28, day of Kalevala, the day of Finnish culture; May 1, day of Finnish work; June 4, day of celebration of Defense Forces; December 6, Independence Day; and days of national and regional elections and the day the president takes office.

The flag also flies officially on Midsummer Day, the Saturday between June 20 and June 26, the day of the Finnish flag. It is raised on Midsummer Eve (Friday) at 6:00 P.M. and stays hoisted all night. It is lowered on Midsummer Day (Saturday) at 9:00 P.M.

The cross—called the Scandinavian cross—appears on the flags of several other countries and territories. Of these, the five official flags are those of Finland, Denmark, Sweden, Norway, and Iceland. They are all based on the cross that decorated the flags of the Crusaders. Each of these flags uses a combination of two or three of the colors white, red, blue, and gold.

Other unofficial flags using the Scandinavian cross include those of the Aland Islands, Faroe Islands, Orkney Islands, and Shetland Islands, all areas populated by Vikings.

began offering land grants and tax relief to many of its soldiers. They called Finland *Österland,* meaning "land to the east," and considered it a province of Sweden. During this time, many Finns retreated to the central part of the country and continued to rebel. Mostly peasant farmers, they eventually lived peacefully with the Swedish landowners and church leaders.

In the meantime, the Russians kept pushing into Finland, sending their Orthodox monks up into Lapland and soldiers to burn the cathedral in Turku. The Swedes responded by building a castle in Vyborg (*Viipuri* in Finnish) in far eastern Finland. In 1323, Sweden and Russia signed a peace treaty agreeing to define the eastern border for the first time. For the next several hundred years, this border would shift between Finland and Russia many times.

Although the Finns were considered part of Sweden, they still maintained an independent spirit. In Europe, a strong nobility ruled over a feudal system, but this did not take hold in Finland. Finnish peasants were self-sufficient and resourceful. They held on to their own language. Many held administrative posts in the Swedish government, were able to vote in Swedish elections (where kings and queens were elected), studied in European universities, and even lived in Stockholm.

During the 1400s, Sweden joined forces with Denmark and Norway to form the Kalmar Union. Finland appeared on a map of the world for the first time and became a more important trade center, attracting foreign merchants interested in furs and fish. By 1523, the Union was dissolved when the Swedes and Finns objected to the harsh taxes and other unfair practices imposed by the Danish. King Gustav Vasa took over the Swedish throne. He established the first national standing army in Europe and adopted the Protestant Lutheran faith. (By then, many Finns had been converted by German missionaries.) In order to increase his military and financial power, King Vasa also took over all the properties of the Catholic Church.

By this time, the Catholics had built stone churches throughout Finland. Decorated with colorful frescos, they were seized by King Vasa's armies and whitewashed. Although the Catholic religion may have faded in Finland in this era, Finnish customs did not. For the first time, the Finnish alphabet was written down, as a bishop named Mikael Agricola (1510–1557) translated parts of the Bible into Finnish in 1539. Earlier he

King Gustav III of Sweden ruled Finland at the height of the Swedish Empire in the seventeenth century.

had studied literature and religion with Martin Luther, the founder of the Lutheran faith, in Germany. In addition to writing the alphabet, he wrote about Finnish culture and religion. Many of the royal family were taught Finnish, and it began to be used in government offices. In 1550, the city of Helsinki was founded on the south coast as a trading post.

During the 1600s, the Swedish Empire reached the peak of its power in a "golden age." The ruling monarchy became more powerful, switching from elected to hereditary rulers. With the most modern army and administration in Europe, the Swedes controlled Finland, Estonia, and parts of Latvia, Denmark, and Germany. Under this government, the Finnish cavalry (*hakkapeliitas*) was feared by European soldiers for its fierce fighting. During the Thirty Years' War (1618–1648), Swedes and Finns fought religious and political battles in Europe. They pushed again into Russia, next to eastern Finland. Many Finnish farmers settled there and the Russians retaliated by burning their homes.

Finland began to grow more during the second half of the seventeenth century. Many new towns were founded as well as a post office, the University of Turku, and the beginnings of Finnish industry: paper mills, iron works, shipbuilding, and tar making (used in building ships). Despite these advances, life for the average Finn (mostly farmers) was still harsh, and Finland was still seen by the rest of the world as a dark land overshadowed by Sweden. According to historian W.R. Mead, three basic facts about Finland emerged at the time when a new map of Finland was introduced:

> . . . that Finland was an integral part of the Scandinavian world, a marshland country afflicted with the recurrent scourge of war and a . . . land in which winter took precedence over summer. It was, in effect, what the

16th century poet Andrew Boode called a "Kingdom of the Night." [5]

SWEDES AND RUSSIANS FIGHT FOR CONTROL

The eighteenth century was a turbulent one in Europe, marked by wars and revolutions that would finally bring an end to Sweden's empire and rule over Finland. From 1700 to 1721, Denmark, Poland, and Russia fought against Sweden in the Great Northern War. During the last seven years of that war, in a period the Finns call the Great Wrath, the Russians destroyed Finland and treated the people harshly, even sending some to Russia as slaves. In 1710, a plague wiped out two-thirds of Helsinki's population. Under Peter the Great, Russia emerged as a strong power and established the city of St. Petersburg at the eastern edge of the Gulf of Finland, replacing a Swedish fort. Sweden was forced to give up much of its empire, including parts of eastern Finland. Twenty years later, Sweden tried to reclaim these areas and the Russians moved in again, in a period called the Lesser Wrath. Again, the Swedes were forced to give up more territory. They worked hard to improve conditions in Finland, however. They built many towns and several fortresses, including a large one on Suomenlinna, an island off Helsinki. Finland's population grew, and many moved into new industrial areas such as Tampere. By this time, both Sweden's government control and Finland's rural economy were suffering. Caught between warring neighbors, the Finns divided into two political groups: the Hats, who wanted Sweden to oppose Russia and control Finland, and the Nightcaps, who wanted to appease Russia.

In the late 1700s, Sweden's King Gustav III won several sea battles against the Russians but regained no territory. Fighting resumed again in 1807 when Russia and France, at war with Britain, tried to force Sweden to close its ports to Britain. When Sweden refused, Alexander I of Russia attacked Finland. For a year, the Finns fought the Russians but were finally defeated in 1809. Sweden was forced to turn over Finland, ending its seven hundred years of rule over Finland.

RUSSIANS

Under the Russian czar Alexander I, Finland became an autonomous grand duchy (a special domain in the Russian Empire). For the first time, Finland was a national entity rather than a group of provinces as it had been under Swedish rule. Fearing that the Finns might be difficult to control, the Russians ruled Finland with a light hand. Many Finns found it easy to accept the transition as they were tired of being caught in wars between their two neighbors. They developed loyalty to the Russian czar.

The Russians in turn allowed the Finns to retain their Swedish system of laws, language, and religion. Although ruled by the czar, the Finns had their own senate and could elect representatives to the Russian assembly. Many Finns had careers in the Russian government and army. In 1812, the Russians moved the capital from Turku on the west coast, where it was close to Sweden, to Helsinki on the south coast, just two hundred miles from St. Petersburg. They also returned parts of eastern Finland to the Finns.

A Finnish clergyman named Adolph Arvidsson tried to encourage Finnish nationalism in the 1820s when he wrote, "Swedes we are not, Russians we will never be, so let us become Finns." [6] His ideas were not popularly supported, and he was forced to move to Sweden. Not until later in the century would the idea of a separate Finnish country begin to grow.

In the meantime, Finland began to develop into a modern industrial country. New industries included sawmills, paper and pulp factories, textile manufacturing, metalworks, and engineering. More people moved to the cities, and the first railroad connected Helsinki with the interior in 1862. Finnish became an official language used in government offices. Everyone was taught to read and write; in fact a new law was passed that required men and women to read before they could marry. Finland also adopted its own currency, the markka, its own postage stamps, and established an army.

In rural areas, life was still harsh. During the 1860s, severe weather and a resulting famine killed one-third of the rural population. More than 320,000 Finns emigrated to the United States and Canada during the next fifty years seeking better living conditions and opportunities to escape poverty. Those farmers and workers who remained began organizing into cooperatives and trade unions. Many of these groups would evolve into the political parties that still play a strong part in Finnish politics today. Some supported socialism, which became the basis of the modern welfare state.

By the turn of the century, Finnish arts and culture were attracting attention at the World's Fair in Paris. A feeling of patriotism and a desire for a national identity was celebrated by many Finnish writers, artists, and musicians.

Despite attempts by the Russian czar Nicholas II to stop this growing feeling of nationalism (he wanted to make Russian the official language and disband the Finnish army), the Finns resisted in a strong, but mostly nonviolent way. In 1906, they pushed for a stronger democracy and established their own parliament. They gave everyone—men and women—the right to vote and to hold political office, thus becoming the first country in the world to grant women full political rights.

Preoccupied by a war with Japan and its own internal conflicts, the Russians went along with Finnish demands. Soon Russia was also pulled into World War I (1914–1918), siding

THE FINLAND-FRIENDLY CZAR

In Helsinki's Senate Square, outside the government buildings, stands a statue of Russian czar Alexander II, who ruled Finland as part of the Russian Empire from 1855 to 1881. His presence puzzles some who wonder why the Finns commemorate a foreign ruler.

Alexander II was the friendliest of the five Grand Dukes who oversaw Finland from 1809 to 1917, when Russia fell to revolutionaries and Finland became independent. Although his uncle, Alexander I, had established Finland's legislative assembly, the Diet, when he took over Finland from Sweden in 1809, it was never allowed to meet during his reign or the subsequent reign of his brother, Nicholas I.

It was Alexander II, son of Nicholas I, who called for regular meetings of the Finnish Diet more than fifty years after it was first established. In doing so, he limited his own powers. He began a campaign of reform and modernization. In Finland this included establishing Finnish as the language of government, the silver mark as Finland's currency (separate from Russia's), freedom of worship, and an independent Finnish army.

In Russia, Alexander's reforms were considered too liberal by reactionaries and too moderate by liberals and radicals. When radicals protested, several hundred of them, mostly students, they were arrested. The radicals retaliated by making several attempts on Alexander's life. They finally succeeded in 1881 when he was assassinated by a hand-thrown bomb.

His son, Alexander III, and grandson, Nicholas II, were the next and last two czars to rule Russia and Finland. By the time Nicholas II took over in 1894, Russia was trying to expand its empire and took away most of Finland's autonomy. The Finnish army was dissolved.

It was during this time that the Finns erected the statue of Alexander II in Senate Square. To them, he stood for a happier time when they enjoyed more freedom. It was a clever form of protest, because Nicholas II could not really prevent the Finns from erecting a statue of his respected and martyred grandfather.

Finnish women were given the right to vote and hold political office in 1906, making Finland the world's first country to grant full woman suffrage.

with Britain, France, and the United States against Germany, Austria-Hungary, Bulgaria, and the Ottoman Empire. Although Russian troops were stationed in Finland, most Finns stayed out of the war. A few who wanted to break away from Russia fought with the Germans. On November 6, 1917, Russia's government was overthrown by communist revolutionaries (Czar Nicholas II had been replaced by a provisional government in March). Finland took advantage of this and declared its independence on December 6. By early 1918, Russia acknowledged Finland as an independent country.

After eight hundred years of foreign occupation, Finland was about to embark on its next journey, transforming itself from a rural to a modern urban nation. The Finns, descended from hardy nomads who first settled their land, were well prepared for this twentieth-century voyage.

FROM FARM AND FOREST TO URBAN HIGH TECH

When Finland became independent from Russia in 1917, more than 70 percent of Finns lived in rural areas. Most relied on farming and forestry to make a living. Today the majority of the Finnish people live in and around urban areas, and many work in new, innovative industries. In less than a hundred years, Finland has transformed itself from a little-known and remote Russian territory to a modern democracy with one of the highest standards of living in the world.

Although in some ways this transformation seemed to happen quickly, it was based on a strong sense of self-reliance and fairness the Finns had cultivated for centuries. This inner strength (known as *sisu*) helped them survive wars, foreign occupation, plagues, famines, a harsh climate, and a remote location. In the twentieth century, it continued to pull them through two world wars and out from under the shadow of Soviet Russia.

INDEPENDENCE AND CIVIL WAR

No sooner had the Finnish people declared their independence on December 6, 1917, when they began fighting each other over the type of government they should adopt. Conservative government forces let by General Carl Mannerheim (1867–1951) started to disarm the Russian troops in western Finland. They were called the White Guards or the Whites. A few of these Whites had fought for the Germans.

In southern Finland, a revolutionary group backed by forty thousand Russian troops tried to seize power. Called the Red Guards, or the Reds, they were inspired by the recent revolution in Russia. Although many of the Whites were poorly trained, they managed to defeat the Reds within a few months, aided by German, Swedish, and Norwegian troops. Before the fighting was over in the spring of 1918, more than thirty thousand had died, more Reds than Whites.

The Whites favored a monarchy and chose a German prince—Friedrich Karl, son-in-law of the German emperor—to be king. Within a month, and before he could even set foot in Finland, he renounced the throne when the Germans were defeated in World War I. For approximately a year, temporary leaders were chosen to lead the country, including General Mannerheim. Finally, in 1919, the Finns established a constitutional republic and elected Kaarlo Juho Stahlberg (1865–1952) as the first president. Stahlberg was a professor of law at the University of Helsinki and president of the Finnish Parliament. He served as president until 1925 and ran again in 1931 and 1937, but was defeated.

German soldiers target Communist snipers in Helsinki during the 1917 civil war. Once the Communist forces were defeated, Finland chose a German prince to be king.

THE GRAND MARSHAL OF FINLAND

One of the most important forces guiding Finland into and through the twentieth century was Carl Gustaf Emil Mannerheim. Today, a statue of Mannerheim astride a horse sits in central Helsinki on a central street named after him. It is both a tribute to the man as a dashing figure and as a leader who helped Finland ride through warring neighbors, civil war, independence, and two world wars.

Mannerheim was born into an elite family north of Turku on the west coast of Finland on June 4, 1867. At the age of fourteen, he was sent to military school but was expelled for disciplinary reasons. Despite this rocky start, he graduated from another school and signed up with the Russian army. He served in regiments in Poland and St. Petersburg and in the Russo-Japanese War of 1904–1905, during which he was promoted to colonel.

The following year, the army sent Mannerheim on a special assignment to study the various tribes and territories along the "silk route." It took Mannerheim two years to travel the eighty-seven hundred miles from Turkestan to Beijing, China. Riding the same horse during the entire journey, he stopped to collect artifacts and take photographs and he even met the Dalai Lama. Later, he wrote about his travels.

Mannerheim was married briefly to a Russian woman and had two daughters. After their divorce, his wife moved to France with their children and Mannerheim did not see them often. Mannerheim's real devotion was to the military and to the emerging nation of Finland. During World War I, he served on the front and was a decorated hero; but when Russia fell to revolutionaries and Finland declared its independence in 1917, Mannerheim quit the Russian army and returned to Finland. He organized the White Guards and, with the help of German troops, fought the Red Guards in Finland's civil war. After winning, he was made regent of Finland. He ran for the presidency but was defeated by a political science professor, K.J. Stahlberg. He then worked behind the scenes for the Red Cross and for the League for Child Welfare, which he founded.

In 1939, in his seventies, Mannerheim was asked to come back into public life. As commander in chief of the armed services, he successfully defended Finland against the Russians for five difficult years. He was appointed president of Finland for two years. He retired in 1946 to Switzerland, where he died in 1951 at the age of eighty-three.

Despite his long and successful public career, Mannerheim remained a somewhat distant and mysterious figure. Finnish filmmaker Renny Harlin (who now works in Hollywood and was married to American actress Geena Davis) is currently working on a movie about Mannerheim's life.

In 1920, Finland joined the League of Nations and signed a treaty with Russia that recognized Finland's independence. By 1922, the Finnish government had established freedom of religion, compulsory education, and military service. Laws were also changed to allow poor farmers and their tenants to buy more land. This helped stimulate the economy and narrow class differences.

During the 1920s and 1930s, Finland began to steer a neutral course in the world. A newly crafted ship of state, it carefully maneuvered between eastern socialism and western democratic capitalism. By the late 1920s, its government was formed by coalitions of political parties rather than by any one party. This coalition was usually a shifting combination of liberal and conservative parties. Both the extreme left-wing Communist and the right-wing Lapua Parties tried to gain power, but both were defeated and for a time banned.

Gradually Finland turned away from Russia and Germany and moved more toward the other western and Nordic countries (Norway, Sweden, and Denmark). Although Finland shared geographical closeness and some history with the Nordic countries, there were differences. The Finnish language is different from the similar Germanic languages of Norway, Sweden, and Denmark. In addition, Norway, Sweden, and Denmark were all monarchies with socialist governments. Finland was not a monarchy and adopted a middle ground between socialism and capitalism, with a more liberal economy than the other Nordic countries.

The economy boomed, and Finland was the only European country to repay its war debts to the United States. Through the 1930s, agriculture was still the backbone of Finland's economy. The economic depression that devastated the United States and other European countries did not affect Finland as severely. Many Finns were migrating to the cities and working in the developing mining and metal industries. The lumber and paper-making industries began to lead the way in growth and development and in lucrative trade with Great Britain. By the late 1930s, Finland's two decades of peaceful growth were interrupted by World War II.

WORLD WAR II

Although Germany and Soviet Russia would soon be fighting each other, in 1939 they signed a secret agreement stating that Finland belonged under Soviet influence. Soon after, Germany, under Adolf Hitler, invaded Poland and started World War II. Finland tried to remain neutral, but the Russians, fueled by their secret agreement, had other ideas. Before the end of the war in 1945, Finland would be drawn into three different wars: the Winter War, the Continuation War, and the Lapland War.

The Winter War began on November 30, 1939, when a million Russian troops attacked Finland in four different parts of the country. Under the Russian dictator Joseph Stalin, the Russians installed a puppet government in Finland and expected Finnish workers and socialists to support them. Instead, most Finns remained loyal to their own government and called the new government an "Asiatic joke." Vastly outnumbered, with little support from the rest of the world, Finnish soldiers under General Mannerheim held off Russian troops for 105 days. Even though they used old weapons, they were more skilled than the Russians at maneuvering and surviving in the frozen forests. One of their favorite weapons was the Molotov cocktail, bottles filled with gasoline, named after a Russian foreign minister they blamed for starting the war.

By March 1940, Stalin decided to abandon the new government and negotiate for peace. Even though his troops were winning, he feared interference from Western countries. By this time, two hundred thousand Soviet and twenty-five thousand Finnish soldiers had died. Finland was forced to give up a tenth of its territory to Russia but remained independent.

A year later, fearing another attack by the Russians, Finland turned to Germany for help, thus beginning the Continuation War (1941–1944). The Finns considered this war to be separate from World War II. They despised Nazi ideology and refused German pressure to deport the few Jewish people in

As Joseph Stalin looks on (third from left), a Soviet official signs a treaty in December of 1939 legitimizing the Soviet invasion of Finland.

Finland to concentration camps. They looked upon Germany as a necessary evil they needed to help them avoid Russian invasion. Germany had already attacked Russia and was occupying France, Sweden, and Denmark.

Despite a massive Russian invasion, the Finnish army, with Germany's help, was able to stand its ground and fight off Russian troops in several parts of the country. The Finns were also able to prevent the bombing of Helsinki with a strong air-defense plan. In September 1944, they signed a peace settlement with Russia. The settlement returned to Finland some of the eastern parts of Finland that Russia had taken over a few years earlier. Overall, the Finns lost more than they gained, however: access to the Arctic Ocean in the north and 30 percent of its hydroelectric power, 12 percent of its forests, 9 percent of its farmland, and many of its mines. In addition, the Russians took over the Porkkala peninsula near Helsinki as a naval base and forced the Finns to pay them $300 million in manufactured goods.

Finnish soldiers fire on the Soviets during World War II. With Germany's help, Finland was able to repel the large-scale Soviet offensive of 1944.

The Russians then pressured Finland to get rid of any remaining German troops. The Germans set fires as they retreated north from the Finnish army in this period called the Lapland War (1944–1945). They left behind a scorched and devastated land. The main city in Lapland—Rovaniemi—was destroyed. Despite this devastation, the Finnish army gained a reputation worldwide for its courage and fighting ability. In 1948, Russian dictator Joseph Stalin acknowledged the strength of the Finnish fighting forces: "Nobody respects a country with a poor army, but everyone respects a country with a good army. I raise my toast to the Finnish Army."[7]

In all, 80,000 Finns died in these three wars. More than 450,000 refugees from Karelia in eastern Finland (10 percent of the population) had to find new homes. About 70,000 children were evacuated to Sweden and Denmark, and about 50,000 people in Lapland were uprooted and moved to Sweden or central Finland. After the war, many of the children and Laplanders were able to return.

POSTWAR RECOVERY

The years directly following World War II were difficult ones for the Finns. Many people were poor and hungry because there were few jobs and little food. Even though they signed a treaty of friendship and cooperation with Russia, they feared a Communist takeover, as had happened in many other Eastern European countries such as Poland, East Germany, Estonia, and Latvia on the other side of the Baltic. The Communist Party did win parliamentary seats and cabinet posts in Finland (including that of prime minister), but, by the late 1940s, its power had declined. In its place, combinations of the Social Democrats (socialistic) and the Agrarian Party (moderately conservative) ran the government.

Russia pressured Finland to reject American Marshall Plan aid used to rebuild many countries such as Japan after the war. As a result, the Finns were on their own again, relying on their stamina, innovation, and determination to succeed. This they did very well, managing to resume their own unique path between East and West.

By the early 1950s, Finnish modern design in architecture, furniture, home accessories, and textiles had attracted worldwide attention. Exports of these products stimulated the economy. In 1952, Helsinki hosted the Olympic Games, and the last train carrying goods to pay off war debts crossed the eastern border into Russia. Finland had paid off its debt to Russia down to the last cent.

In 1955, Finland moved more into the world, joining the United Nations and the Nordic Council. The purpose of the Nordic Council was to promote the special interests of Sweden, Norway, Denmark, Iceland, and Finland. Its underlying agenda was the development of the welfare-state model. With the help of the baby boom in the postwar years, Finland's population continued to grow and shift from rural to urban areas.

Finland also continued to cultivate beneficial trade and political relationships with other Nordic and European countries and with Russia. The Finnish army purchased equipment from both Eastern and Western countries, equipping Soviet airplanes, for example, with Western electronics. The Finnish media kept a low profile, censoring itself so as not to offend neighboring capitalists or Communists.

In 1956, Russia returned the Porkkala naval base and a charismatic Finnish politician—Urho Kekkonen—was elected as president. During the next twenty-five years, until 1981, he would be reelected three more times, making him Finland's longest-serving president. Under his strong leadership, Finland moved forward despite its uneasy alliance with the Soviets.

At least twice, the Soviets interfered directly in Finnish affairs. In one incident, the Russians tried in 1958 to change the composition of the government. In another incident a few years later, they interfered directly in an election. By the late 1960s, the term *Finlandization* had been coined to describe a foreign policy of neutrality that makes a non-Communist country susceptible to the influence of the Communist Soviet Union.

FROM SMALL FARMS TO URBAN INDUSTRIES

Finland's economy continued to grow rapidly and change from one based on small farms to one based on urban industries. Farms and fishing centers became bigger and more businesslike. The wood processing, metal, and engineering industries also grew. As Finland developed its welfare state and government planning expanded, related service agencies also grew, employing more people. Despite the expansion of the welfare state and increasing regulation in all areas of life, an economy based on capitalistic market principles prevailed.

Although Russia tried to pressure Finland to withdraw from the Nordic Council, Finland continued to move into international markets. In 1973, they signed a free-trade agreement with

THE COLD WAR PRESIDENT

Finland's longest-serving president was Urho Kekkonen. A charismatic leader, he helped guide Finland through twenty-five of the difficult Cold War years when hostilities increased between Soviet Russia and the West.

Although he has been criticized for inviting a close political and economic relationship with Russia and for using his power to influence domestic affairs (dissolving parliament several times, for example), he is also credited with keeping Finland on a peaceful and prosperous path. As president from 1956 to 1982, he helped Finland survive under the giant shadow of Soviet Russia next door, while the rest of the Western world feared a Communist takeover. He was sometimes called the "Weather Vane," as attuned as he was to the surrounding political winds.

Kekkonen's life spanned almost nine decades of the twentieth century. He was born in 1900 in the rural area of Eastern Finland, the son of a farmworker (later a forestry manager) and a farmer's daughter. He did well in school and planned to be a writer. When the Finnish civil war erupted in 1917, Kekkonen became a war correspondent representing the White troops in Eastern Finland. After the war, he moved to Helsinki where he studied law and began writing for several publications. He was also an athlete—a high jumper—and became involved in several sports organizations, including the Finnish Olympic Committee. In 1926, he married Finnish writer Sylvi Uino.

After visiting Germany in the early 1930s and being repelled by Hitler's rise to power, he warned of the possible threat of the extreme right. He did not like the extreme left either (the Communist Party had been banned in Finland) and so joined the middle-of-the-road Agrarian Party. It was from this vantage point that he moved into politics, becoming a member of parliament and minister of the interior. During World War II, he directed the welfare center for the Karelian refugees. In the years following the war, Kekkonen became Finland's prime minister and minister of foreign relations.

In 1956, he was elected president. In addition to guiding Finland through the Cold War era and encouraging economic development, he hosted the Conference on Security and Cooperation in 1975. This was a meeting of thirty-five countries, which drew up agreements (known as the Helsinki Accords) on human rights and freedoms, military security, and the sharing of economic, environmental, scientific, and humanitarian resources. He considered this the highlight of his career. He died in 1986.

President Urho Kekkonen governed Finland during much of the Cold War.

the European Economic Community (EEC), a forerunner of the European Union (EU). Two years later, they signed the Helsinki Accords, along with the United States, Russia, and more than thirty other countries. These agreements defined human rights, military security, and the sharing of economic, environmental, scientific, and humanitarian resources.

During this period of détente (a lessening of Cold War tensions between East and West), the Communist Party lost influence in Finland, splitting into factions. But the government did not veer too far to the right either. Student radicals, trade union, and agri-

HIGH-TECH SUCCESS STORY

One of Finland's best success stories is Nokia, a world leader in high-tech wireless communications. In the last 20 years, Nokia has entered and pulled ahead in the growing telecommunications markets and is now the number-one manufacturer of wireless phones. Nokia's history, however, goes back 138 years to another mode of communication: paper.

It began in 1865 when an engineer named Fredrik Idestam established a wood-pulp mill in a little town called Nokia on a river in southern Finland. Its purpose was to make paper and cardboard, then in great demand. The community of Nokia, with its work force and hydroelectricity, attracted other companies, such as the Finnish Rubber Works. Manufacturers of galoshes, raincoats, tires, rubber bands, and industrial parts, they began using the name Nokia.

After World War II, Nokia bought Finnish Cable Works, manufacturers of cable for telegraph and telephone networks. By the 1960s, electronic, computer, and network technology became more sophisticated and Nokia was at the forefront. They developed a digital switch to replace the electromechanical analog switches. They developed telephone network software. During the 1980s, Nokia acquired several telecommunications and consumer-electronics companies in Sweden, Germany, and France. They also bought a cable machinery company in Switzerland, a cable company in the Netherlands, and a data-systems division of rival Ericsson in Sweden.

Although the company had expanded into manufacturing other products, such as televisions, it was the telecommunications division that rode out the recession of the early 1990s. The company then decided to focus on promoting its cell phones. When they introduced their first model, the 2100, in 1994, they hoped to sell five hundred thousand of them. They sold 20 million. Since then, Nokia has become the world's number-one manufacturer of cell phones.

In recent years, despite another recession and more cutbacks, Nokia remains a pioneering force in the high-tech world. The company is now moving into third-generation wireless technologies that make sending e-mails and pictures faster and cheaper. They are also moving into other countries such as China, the world's biggest wireless market.

cultural organizations criticized uncontrolled corporate growth and demonstrated for workers' rights. The work week was reduced to forty hours.

By the 1980s, Finland was a strong industrialized democracy and a leader in health care, environmental planning, and social and gender equality. With a booming economy, it was called the Japan of Europe. By the late 1980s, the Conservative Party took over with the election of a conservative prime minister Harri Holkeri. For the first time, the Centre Party was the opposing party.

Much of the booming economy depended on trade with Russia. In exchange for Russian oil, which kept oil prices down, Finland traded forestry and metal products, textiles, and clothing. Other aspects of the economy, called "casino" economics, were based on real estate and stock market speculation. These came crashing down in the early 1990s, along with the Soviet Union. For Finland, the economic recession of 1991–1993 was the severest in its history. Although Russia now recognized Finland as an equal (the old treaty of 1948 was allowed to lapse), they were no longer able to offer lucrative trade. Finland suffered from major bank failures, very high unemployment, currency devaluation, budget deficits, and an inability to pay business loans. Some public services were cut back as criticisms of the state welfare system increased.

Under President Martti Ahtisaari, from 1994 to 2000, the Finns worked hard and turned their economy around. At home, they focused on reducing unemployment and developing their design and engineering skills in new technologies. Beyond their borders, they increased trade with Western countries, joining the EU in 1995. They increased trade with Sweden, acquiring mutual companies. In 2002, they began using the euro currency.

Throughout the rest of the 1990s and the beginning of the twenty-first century, Finland's new industries created higher employment and a dynamic economy. One of its most famous pioneers is Linus Torvalds, creator of the Linux computer operating system. And Nokia, developer of wireless technology and the leading manufacturer of cell phones, is located in Finland.

FINLAND TODAY

Compared to the beginning of the twentieth century, the distribution of Finland's population and work has reversed itself. Whereas in 1900 about 70 percent of the people lived in rural areas and 30 percent in urban areas, now 70 percent live in cities and 30 percent in rural areas. A hundred years ago, most Finns relied on farming and forestry to make a living. Now less than 10 percent do so. The majority of Finns today work in industrial and service jobs.

Although Finnish women have not served in parliament or held cabinet posts since 1906, one is now leading the government for the first time. In 2000, the Finnish people elected their first woman president, Tarja Halonen.

The recent worldwide economic slump has slowed Finland's economic growth somewhat. Many businesses—including divisions of Nokia—have had to cut jobs. The unemployment rate is high (9.1 percent in 2002). There are disagreements within the government about Finland's future course. Some want to continue on a neutral course. Some want to align themselves with defense-oriented members of the EU and the North Atlantic Treaty Organization (NATO).

Although Finland, like the rest of the world, faces many uncertainties in this new century, it remains a strong democracy with one of the world's highest standards of living. The fact that it has survived so well offers hope to other small countries facing obstacles. According to historian Fred Singleton:

> Finland's greatest contribution to twentieth-century civilization, however, lies simply in the fact that it has survived intact as a nation state dedicated to the principles of parliamentary democracy and that it has been able to maintain a welfare state with a high (and steadily rising) national living standard, despite the battering it has endured from a hostile world during the brief period of its national independence. The hope which Finland's example gives to small nations faced with apparently overwhelming odds is Finland's greatest contribution to human welfare. [8]

High Ideals on Solid Ground

Finland's transformation in the last century from a rural Russian territory to a sophisticated, modern nation has been a rapid, even an amazing, one. This transformation has not occurred easily or miraculously, however. It has taken years of hard work to build a solid structure: a democratic government, a welfare state, a strong economy, innovative technology, and an efficient infrastructure. It has also taken a constant commitment to high ideals, especially the idea that each citizen deserves a decent standard of living. This winning combination of high ideals on solid ground allows both—as in a good marriage—to thrive.

GOVERNMENT

Finland is a republic. A republic is a government with a chief of state, usually a president as opposed to a monarch, and in which supreme power resides in its citizens who elect representatives to govern for them based on constitutional law. Every Finnish citizen at least eighteen years of age can vote in presidential and parliamentary elections. The government in Finland includes three branches: executive, legislative, and judicial. These three branches share a balance of power.

The executive branch of the government includes a president, a prime minister, and a cabinet of ministers. The president is elected every six years directly by the people. He or she can serve up to two six-year terms. The president is considered the chief of state and a symbol of the unity of the nation. The president introduces or vetoes legislation, determines foreign policy, oversees the military and defense policies, nominates or appoints certain officials, and represents the country by appearing and speaking in public. The current president is Tarja Halonen. She was elected for the first time in February 2000 and can run again if she decides to in February 2006.

Finland's parliament building stands in Helsinki. Finland's government features a unicameral parliament with two hundred members.

The prime minister is elected by parliament after the parliamentary elections every four years and is then formally appointed by the president. The prime minister is the head of the government and works closely with a cabinet of ministers. Together, the prime minister and the cabinet of ministers are called the council of state. Many prime ministers are former heads of political parties or have held another office such as speaker of the parliament. The current prime minister is Matti Vanhanen. He took office in June 2003.

The cabinet ministers head various departments of the government, or ministries, including the Ministry of Social Affairs and Health, Ministry of the Environment, Ministry of Defense, and Ministry of the Interior. Ministers are nominated by the president and approved by the parliament. They are responsible to parliament. Many members of parliament (MPs) also serve as ministers at the same time. The cabinet can include up to eighteen ministers. Currently there are thirteen.

The president shares power with the legislative branch of government. This is the Eduskunta: a unicameral (one-house) parliament with two hundred members. The MPs are elected by popular vote on a proportional basis every four years. They can serve an unlimited number of four-year terms. The parliament is responsible for passing laws, debating and approving the budget, and supervising the government of the country. The Finnish parliamentary system is based on pragmatic compromise and consensus. For new legislation to be adopted, at least two-thirds of parliament must agree, and for a change in the constitution to take effect, five-sixths must agree. Since there are several political parties in Finland, they often form coalition governments where more than one party shares power. In this way, no one political ideology or program dominates.

The judicial branch of Finland's government is based on modified Swedish law and is overseen by the Ministry of Justice. The president appoints all judges, who must be approved by parliament. There are two main types of courts in Finland: the courts of justice where civil and penal cases are heard, and the administrative courts where cases relating to insurance, business, labor, and similar issues are heard. Each of these has a supreme court, local courts, and regional courts of appeal. Finnish courtrooms are very simple and informal. The judges wear no special robes, and many cases are handled with only written documents. Finnish judges seldom make public appearances.

Finland's Defense Forces include an army, navy, and air force. Every Finnish male eighteen and older is required to serve from six months to a year in the military or community service. Since 1995, women can also serve. The Defense Forces serve under the chief of defense who is directly accountable

Finland's current prime minister, Matti Vanhanen, took office in June 2003. Parliament elects a prime minister every four years.

to the president. In addition, the Frontier Guard (border control), Sea Guard (coast guard), and police force operate under the Ministry of the Interior, although local police are supervised by provincial authorities and are organized into rural and town districts.

A WELFARE STATE

Finland's system of social welfare helps each citizen maintain a decent standard of living. Common to all the Nordic countries,

PARTY POLITICS

In Finland, several political parties vie for political representation. After each parliamentary election, the party with the most votes often forms a coalition government with the runners-up, thus sharing power.

The Finnish party system started in the 1860s when various groups began promoting their interests. Although these parties have taken new forms and new names since Finland became independent in 1917, their basic ideologies have remained constant.

Currently the major parties receiving the most votes in the 2003 parliamentary elections include: Finnish Centre Party (24.7 percent of votes); Social Democratic Party (24.5 percent); National Coalition Party (18.6 percent); Left Alliance (9.9 percent); Green League (8.0 percent); Christian Democrats (5.3 percent); Swedish People's Party (4.6 percent); and True Finns (1.6 percent).

The current prime minister—Matti Vanhanen of the Centre Party—now heads a coalition government consisting of the parliamentary representatives of the Finnish Centre Party, the Social Democratic Party, and the Swedish People's Party.

The Finnish Centre Party was founded in 1906 as the Agrarian Party by rural landowners in northern and eastern Finland. In 1963, it became the Centre Party, to attract people moving to the cities. In the 1990s, it became the Finnish Centre Party, to appeal to people across the whole country. It is considered moderately conservative.

The Social Democratic Party was founded in 1899 as the Finnish Labour Party. When it changed its name to the Social Democratic Party in 1903, it was aligned with Marxist socialists. After the civil war ended in 1918, the most radical left wing of the party fled to Russia and formed the Finnish Communist Party. The remaining Social Democrats continued as a socialistic party.

The National Coalition Party grew out of Finland's earliest party: the Finnish Party, which emerged in the 1860s as part of the Finnish nationalist movement. It is considered moderately conservative, but more conservative than the Centre Party.

The Swedish Party was founded in the 1870s to represent the Swedish-speaking elite in Finland. After a parliament was formed in 1906, it became the Swedish People's Party, to represent all Swedish-speaking people in Finland. It is a middle-of-the-road party.

this system emerged after World War II. By the end of the 1950s, Sweden, Norway, and Denmark had adopted this system, followed by Finland in the 1960s. It is called the "institutional" welfare model and is based on the idea that social welfare benefits should be institutionalized so that all citizens can enjoy a reasonable level of welfare and security. This is in contrast to the "marginal" welfare model, which is based on the idea that only those who can prove need should receive benefits.

Proponents of the institutional welfare model believe that the welfare of the individual is the responsibility of the collective and should be achieved by social and political means rather than by financial markets. It includes constant negotiation and compromise between labor and free-market capital, between employees and employers who together oversee welfare legislation and various programs (such as job training). It also includes the belief—not shared by all—that this social engineering can cure social ills such as poverty and crime.

Finland's welfare institutions cover many parts of life, including education, health, housing, and family. Finland spends less than the other Nordic countries on its welfare programs and is less reform-minded than Sweden. Finland also has less publicly-owned housing in the towns than Sweden does, with more housing benefits going to people in rural areas. Some of Finland's occupational programs are funded by private insurance companies.

The same system of compromise that works in Finland's government also strengthens its welfare state. Currently the middle-of-the-road Centre Party dominates the government, but working with the support of the liberal Social Democrats and other parties keeps the system from being radically reduced or changed.

Finland's welfare system does not come without a price. The Finns pay high income taxes and live with many regulations. When the economy is not good, some services are cut back. Despite their commitment to a decent standard of living for all and a society with no extremes of wealth or poverty, new extremes are emerging, from rich young entrepreneurs to underpaid immigrants and foreign workers. Many wonder how the welfare state will fare as it adjusts to changes in the new global economy.

ECONOMY

Finland's economy is based on the same principles of cooperation and balance that benefit its government and welfare model. It is a blend of socialism and capitalism, with a more market-based economy than in the other Nordic countries. This has encouraged growth, making Finland a highly industrialized country with a per capita output equal to that of Great Britain, France, Germany, or Italy.

In addition to working cooperatively, the Finns work hard and innovatively. In the last fifty years, their economy has shifted from one based on agriculture and forestry to one based on services and manufacturing. The three main manufacturing areas are paper and chemical by-products from wood, metals and engineering, and telecommunications and electronics. Together these account for about 34 percent of Finland's gross domestic product (GDP). Agriculture now accounts for about 4 percent of Finland's GDP. Crops and products are basic: dairy cattle, fish, barley, wheat, potatoes, and sugar beets.

The Finnish economy is dependent on export trade, which makes up a third of its GDP. The Finns export machinery, electronics, chemicals, metals, timber, paper, and pulp to Germany, the United States, Britain, Sweden, Russia, and France. With very few raw materials and energy sources, they import oil from Russia. Most likely, trade with Russia will continue to increase. Currently the Russians are lobbying to build a fifth nuclear reactor in Finland.

In the last ten years, Finland's economy has had its ups and downs. Like many other industrialized countries, Finland experienced a recession in the early 1990s. Finland's was made even worse by the collapse of the Soviet Union, their main trading partner at the time. By the mid-1990s, the Finnish economy was booming again, the result of high-tech successes such as Nokia and the nation's joining the EU.

Since the 2001 terrorist attacks in the United States, the war in Iraq, and another worldwide recession, Finland's economy has slowed down again. Finnish bankers predicted a low (or even nonexistent) growth rate for 2003 and a possible unemployment rate of 9.3 percent. There has been a decline in imports and exports and an increase in job layoffs as many companies, including Nokia, streamlined their operations.

As of August 2003, the unemployment rate was 9.1 percent. Predictions for 2004 are cautiously optimistic. The current government has promised to promote employment, entrepreneurship, and a common solidarity; to increase taxes on energy and environment; and to increase child allowances and decrease income taxes.

Stevedores load cargo for export (below) as a cargo ship docks at a commercial port in Helsinki (left). Finland's economy is heavily dependent on export trade.

TECHNOLOGY

Although the Finns believe in working cooperatively, they are also independent thinkers with a flair for innovative design. In the last fifty years, they have applied this innovative talent to make the best use of their limited natural resources. According to historian Fred Singleton in *A Short History of Finland:*

> The secret of Finland's success has been its ability to specialize in the production of goods and services which make best use of its limited material resources. [Ralph Waldo] Emerson might have been writing about Finland when he said "If a man write a better book, preach a better sermon, or make a better mouse-trap than his neighbour, though he build his house in the woods, the world will make a beaten path to his door." Finland's "better mouse-traps" include ice-breakers, glassware, ceramics, pharmaceutical products, high-quality textiles, prefabricated houses, sports equipment, electronics, cruise liners and a whole host of other specialized products in which skill, design, originality and flair account for more than bulk, volume and mass-production capacity.[9]

Rather than trying to compete with European or American countries that rely on quantity to succeed, the Finns emphasize quality. They have applied this in every industry, from forestry to electronics. They have invented new methods of extracting pulp and chemical by-products from wood to become leaders in paper manufacturing. They excel at making computerized mechanical systems and rifles. (Their gun manufacturer Sako—pronounced "socko"—is one of the best known, with a reputation for accuracy.) They also make high-quality, reliable snowmobiles and icebreaker ships and beautiful textiles, furniture, ceramics, and home accessories.

In the last ten to fifteen years, the Finns have moved happily and successfully into the world of wireless communications and related industries as companies like Nokia have developed and adapted new designs, technologies, and equipment. According to a report issued in February 2003 by the World Economic Forum, Finland was number one (out of eighty-two countries examined) in its use and application of information and communication technologies (ICT):

> The Finnish public, the business community and public authorities have the highest state of readiness for the use and application of ICT, a desirable condition also known as networked readiness. [10]

This innovation on the part of Finnish industries shows no signs of slowing down. According to British geography professor W.R. Mead of University College in London, Finland's myths do not include a golden age, so its people look to the future rather than the past. The most recent generation, he says, is Finland's happiest and is not given to nostalgia: "Finland is a nation with a cadre of energetic scientists, engineers and technicians who look to the future and who are bent on advancing the status that the country has already achieved." [11]

INFRASTRUCTURE

The same hard work and commitment to excellent design that have built a strong government and economy have also helped the Finns build a strong, efficient infrastructure. It is now possible to travel almost anywhere in Finland on a paved highway. Most of the country's 30,937 miles of highway are two lanes wide. There are approximately 275 miles of wider expressways. Except for the commuters who travel between Helsinki and its outlying suburbs, most Finns encounter very light traffic. In rural areas, the Finns are required to drive with their headlights on even in the daytime. Wandering reindeer in the far north, especially near tourist areas, and wandering moose everywhere else in Finland, are the main hazards. According to travel writers Jennifer Brewer and Markus Lehtipuu:

> Your average reindeer—none too swift to begin with— is totally blasé about many signs of civilization— including, sadly, oncoming cars. Some 3000 to 4500 reindeer die annually on Finnish roads, and trains kill an additional 600 every year. . . . Reindeer move slowly and do not respond to car horns. Nor do they seem to feel that automobiles deserve right of way. [12]

In addition to its highways, Finland has 3,644 miles of excellent railroads, offering fast, dependable service between major cities. Its three main lines travel north and south, connecting with less frequent east-to-west trains. Buses also travel over 90 percent of Finland's roads and are used for traveling to smaller towns and villages.

More than half of Finland's 4,148 miles of waterways are suitable for large ships, including those that travel up the Russian-owned Saimaa Canal from the Gulf of Finland into the Lake District. Originally steamboats carried goods and people in this area. Now a few have been taken out of retirement and are used as tourist attractions. In the summer, many Finns rely on modern ferries to take them through Finland's interconnected lakes and rivers. It is possible to cover half of the country this way, and many take their bicycles with them. Free ferries— considered part of the highway system—also connect many offshore islands with the mainland. These ferries carry pedestrians, cars, and bicycles. Finland has some of the best bicycle paths and pedestrian walkways in the world. It is not unusual to see pedestrians skiing along these paths in the winter and even in the summer using special skis with wheels.

Finland has eleven ports and harbors, a fleet of ninety-eight merchant marine ships, and a fleet of nine icebreaker ships that can move through great walls of ice, keeping the waterways open even in the winter. In addition to local ferries, international ferries, catamarans, and hydrofoils operate regularly between Finland and Estonia, Sweden, Germany, and Russia. Finland's two main cruise lines are the Viking Line and the Silja (Seal) Line.

Finland's state-owned airline, Finnair, flies throughout Finland and the world. A newer, privately owned airline, Flying Finn, flies throughout Finland and to a few European cities. For shorter flights, the Finns rely on Karair, its charter airline. The country has 160 airports, 74 with paved runways.

Finland's roads, railways, and waterways are serving the Finnish people and their country well. So far, their neutral path in world politics has also worked for them. Today, however, many Finns are questioning if this neutral role will continue to work.

ROLE IN WORLD POLITICS

In 1871, Finnish writer Zacharias Topelius described how he thought Finland should appear to the world. Finland's goal, he said, is "to be neutral, to be self-sufficient, to have the freedom to look after one's own interests." [13]

More than 130 years later, Finland is much better known in the world than it was then. Yet is has managed to become so without sacrificing its policy of neutrality or its freedom. In fact, it is the policy of neutrality itself that has helped Finland succeed in the world. Because the Finns have tried to remain neutral in international conflicts, they are well liked around the world. Many have worked as missionaries and in peacekeeping forces for the United Nations. Because they have never had an empire or an ulterior motive in helping others, they have been welcomed into many third world countries. According to historian Fred Singleton: "When Finns become involved in the affairs of the Third World, they do so without means of an imperial past to cloud their relationship with the peoples of Asia and Africa." [14]

Currently Finnish experts are being asked to look for and investigate mass graves in Iraq. In addition to working in other countries, the Finns have hosted many important international conferences and peace summits. These have earned the Finnish a reputation as champions of human rights and active peacekeepers. According to historian Jukka Nevakivi, the Finns have been able to maintain their policy of neutrality without sacrificing strength or independence:

> The neutrality policy, characterized as "active peacekeeping," which Finland has pursued since the beginning of the 1970s has nevertheless obtained results which could not even have been dreamed about in the

FINLAND'S FIRST WOMAN PRESIDENT

Finland's current president—Tarja Halonen—was elected in February 2000. She is Finland's eleventh president and the first woman to hold the job. She is the third Finnish president to come from a Social Democratic background and, according to business writer Deborah Swallow in *Culture Shock: A Guide to Customs and Etiquette: Finland*, "probably the most left-wing head of state the nation has ever had."

Halonen has been described as idealistic yet practical, generous yet demanding, and free-spirited with a good sense of humor. She has been putting her political beliefs to work for more than forty years.

Born in a poor, working-class neighborhood of Helsinki on December 24, 1943, Halonen suffered from a serious speech impediment during her childhood. It still affects her today and has contributed to her sensitivity toward those who are different, her desire to help others, and her concern for human rights and minority issues. A single mother, she raised her daughter alone before marrying a senior civil servant.

After earning a law degree, she was a trade union lawyer for several years before becoming the prime minister's parliamentary secretary in 1974. From there, she moved into several board of director positions for companies and organizations, including the Helsinki City Council. By 1979, she was an MP. By the late 1980s, she moved into the Ministry of Social Affairs and Health. In 1989, she became the minister for Nordic cooperation and, in 1990, the minister of justice. In 1995, she became the first woman to serve as Finland's minister of foreign affairs, a position she held up until her election to the presidency.

Since taking office, Halonen has become even better known for her down-to-earth style and lack of formality. With a strong interest in the theater and the arts, she has promoted cultural as well as social issues. Her approval ratings have remained high among the Finnish people. According to a recent article in the *Helsingin Sanomat,* she is the most popular president Finland has ever had. Her term lasts until 2006, when she can run again if she wants to.

Tarja Halonen celebrates her 60th birthday. Aside from being Finland's first women president, Halonen has become the most popular president in Finland's history.

1950s and 1960s. It has increased Finland's international standing and strengthened its position between East and West. In contrast with earlier times, when Finland drifted into dependency on either East or West if it was confronted by danger, it is at present at a safe distance from both—as distant as it is possible to be in the modern world. And Finland is correspondingly more independent than ever before. [15]

One of Finland's challenges in coming years will be to keep examining and defining its policy of neutrality now that it is a member of the EU. Finland does not belong to NATO, an international organization established in 1949 for purposes of collective security. Several EU countries want to form another similar organization for the purposes of common defense. The Finns are divided about joining this.

In the meantime, from its roads and its waterways to its government and economy, Finland has combined the best of a solid structure and idealistic values. Even in a cold, remote corner of the world, the Finns have proven that it is possible to live well. According to W.R. Mead, "They have demonstrated that the cold periphery of Europe is . . . capable of being transformed into a temperate zone of wellbeing." [16]

Never Far from the Forest

The Finns are never far from the forest. Physically, forests cover most of the land. Even in the cities, the forests are nearby and sometimes even part of the urban landscape. In spirit, these ancient forests are never far from the hearts of the Finnish people either. The forest is as much a part of their character as it is of their land. It has helped them nurture a respect for privacy, nature, and each other. It has also provided them with the freedom to hunt, to explore, and to develop a strong sense of personal and national independence. In modern times, the Finns have built one of the most advanced countries in the world, but the primitive call of the forest is still with them. This is described by Aarne Reunala of the Institute of Forest Research in his essay "The Forest and the Finns": "The old values of the forest are still living in the mind of the modern, even the urban, Finn. Finns are hunters and pioneers, they seek protection in the forest, where they experience an ancient pantheistic union with nature, and the dark conifers and light broad-leafed forests arouse in them feelings of patriotism." [17]

The Finnish Character

Like their forests, the Finns can appear mysterious and full of interesting contrasts. They are at the same time reserved and fun loving, humble and innovative, peaceful and patriotic, cooperative and suspicious of foreigners, law-abiding and fiercely independent.

The characteristic most used to describe the Finnish people is *reserved*. In public they are quiet and seldom smile or show physical affection. They do not like small talk and can seem blunt when they do talk. In private, however, with friends and family, the Finns are fun loving and able to laugh at themselves. They love music, dancing, and a good party.

The Finns are also humble people. Partly fostered by their classless society, they hate to stand out from one another.

A Finnish father holds his son. Though often reserved in public Finns are lively and outgoing amongst family and friends.

Bragging or calling attention to oneself is considered impolite. Even students will avoid asking questions in a classroom so as not to appear rude. Despite this humility, the Finns are great innovators. Their talent for designing new products has helped make them leaders in many modern industries, especially wireless communications.

The Finnish people value peace and have tried to remain neutral in world conflicts and wars. They have hosted several peace summits and have participated in peacekeeping missions. When attacked, however, the Finns have fought valiantly to defend themselves. They are patriotic and participate in elections, with up to 80 percent voting.

Since earlier, rural days when farmers helped one another build houses and clear fields, the Finns have practiced *talkoot* (TAHL-koot), which refers to neighbors helping each other. Today they believe that the government should help people build a just and humane society. Although they have many rules and regulations to ensure this cooperative way of living, they do not seem to mind following them. They consider themselves to be self-reliant, courageous, and fiercely independent.

In fact, the trait the Finns claim to describe themselves—*sisu*—means courage, strength, resilience, determination not to give up in the face of obstacles, and even stubbornness beyond all reason. As travel writers Jennifer Brewer and Markus Lahtipuu describe it: "Even if all looks lost, until the final defeat, a Finn with sisu will fight—or swim, or run, or work—valiantly." [18]

POPULATION DEMOGRAPHICS

Most of Finland's 5.5 million people (93 percent) are descended from Finno-Ugrian tribes, making it one of the most homogeneous countries in the world. Current scientific evidence suggests that these people came from around the Ural Mountains in Russia and moved first into Europe and then north into Finland. Most Finns are slightly darker and shorter than their

THE MYTH OF THE WORLD TREE

Finland's deep and mysterious forests have been a rich source of income for centuries. They have also inspired many myths, such as the one described by Aarne Reunala, director of the Institute of Forest Research, in his essay "The Forest and the Finns" in *Finland: People, Nation, State.* According to Reunala, early Finns saw the universe as being held up by a mighty "world tree." They echoed this belief inside their houses by holding up curved roofs with a strong center pole, which represented the world tree.

Numerous customs have arisen throughout the world from the myth of the world tree. The tree has a central and benevolent part in them. In a religious ceremony the spirit of the bear killed by the hunter was sent to the bears' heaven along the pine where its skull was hung up. Special memorial trees or other sacred trees, which were common in eastern Finland as late as the nineteenth century, protected the household and brought good luck. Damage to them would be followed by misfortune. In the middle of the burnbeaten clearing, the farmer might leave a tree to protect the land's fertility. And wooden objects, foliage and branches were used in numerous spells for curing disease, protecting people and domestic animals, bringing good luck in hunting and fishing, and arousing affection.

The tradition of the world tree has remained alive to the present day. In Sweden and Aland Islands a decorated pole is raised on Midsummer Day. The fire, smoke and ashes of the Midsummer and Easter bonfires have provided protection from spirits and from disease, and in the ceremony of dancing round the fire, the rotation of the universe around its axis, the world tree, is repeated. The Christmas tree dates from the seventeenth century, creating primarily for urban dwellers a new bond with nature and the natural, age-old world system. By bringing an evergreen tree indoors at the darkest time of the year people take a ritual part in the course of the seasons and confirm the coming of the new spring and summer.

The well-known act of "touching wood" may also have its origin in belief in the world tree. The close association of tree and humans is depicted also in the planting of trees to honour significant events and perhaps even in speaking of the genealogical family tree.

Nordic neighbors, and many have high cheekbones. Genetically they are related mostly to Europeans but partly to Asians.

About 350,000 Swedish people live in Finland, most of whom are taller and blonder. Other groups include about 6,000 Saami and 4,000 Gypsies. The exact physical or genetic origin of the Saami, the reindeer herders who gradually migrated north into Lapland, is not yet known. In recent years, immigrants from other countries have been moving into Finland, including Vietnamese, Somalis, and Russians.

More than two-thirds of the Finnish people (67 percent) are between the ages of fifteen and sixty-four. Another 18 percent are fourteen and younger, and 15 percent are sixty-five and older. Finland's birthrate is 10.8 per 1,000 people, and its death rate is 9.73 per 1,000 people. Its population growth rate is .17 percent. This is low compared to 0.89 percent for the United States and means the population will continue to decline in the coming years.

A Saami woman feeds her reindeer. The geographic and genetic origin of the Saami people remains a mystery.

TYPICAL JOBS

Almost a third of Finns (32 percent) work in public services, which include government agencies, health care, and education. The next largest group (22 percent) works in industry, mainly technology, engineering, and paper manufacturing. The rest work in commerce (14 percent); finance, insurance, and business services (10 percent); agriculture and forestry (8 percent); transport and communications (8 percent); and construction (6 percent).

Bolstered partly by the welfare state and by strong employee labor unions and other organizations, Finnish workers enjoy fair wages, generous vacations, and good pension plans. If necessary, they are also entitled to disability pensions and unemployment insurance.

The Finns carry their polite reserve into the work world. They work hard, but follow realistic deadlines (with the exception of the more high-pressure, high-tech jobs). They think of every job as deserving of respect. Workers that in many parts of the world expect tips (such as cabdrivers or waiters) do not in Finland. There is not a strong tradition of philanthropy in Finland because of the high level of government support and lower level of poverty.

FAMILY LIFE

The Finns place a strong value on family ties, more so than material possessions. They tend to put off getting married until they can find an equal partner. Many are choosing not to marry at all. According to a 1999 report, the average age for marriage in Finland has gone up about four years since 1980, to 30.5 for men and 28.3 for women. Most families have two children.

Finnish families prefer eating their meals together. These are usually home cooked rather than fast foods. Most Finnish mothers are employed, and yet they still do more than half of the household tasks. The divorce rate in Finland is high. According to one source, it is the third highest in the world after Russia and Sweden. Finnish women have been more open in recent years in asking for emotional expression from Finnish men.

Government benefits offer generous support for Finnish families. These include pre- and postnatal health care, paid maternity leave (up to ten months, which parents can take separately or split between them), monthly payments for children up to age seventeen, and free day-care centers for children up to age six. In addition, the Finns believe in taking care of the elderly, and the government offers special services for them, including cleaning, cooking, transportation, and nursing homes.

Summer vacations are an important part of Finnish family life. For up to six weeks every year, most get away to their summer house or cabin in the country. (About 25 percent of Finns own summer houses, and the rest can rent them.) They return to their forests for solitude and renewal.

THE ROLE OF WOMEN

Women play an important part in Finland's political and economic life. The current president, Tarja Halonen, is a woman. In addition, the government includes several women ministers and MPs. Many Finnish women also direct companies or head trade unions or university departments. Women make up about half of Finland's workforce, and, about 30 percent of Finnish workers have a woman as a boss. Approximately 58 percent of Finnish women are employed, and of these, 71 percent work full-time—more than in any other European country.

Women in Finland are much less likely to live in poverty than in other parts of the world because of better wages, free day care, and child allowances. According to the Luxembourg Income Study, 2–3 percent of Finnish women are poor, compared to 15 percent in the United States. Even single mothers do better, with 5 percent living in poverty in Finland compared to 45 percent in the United States. Most single mothers in Finland work. According to the study, "Finnish and Swedish single mothers have the highest employment rates and lowest poverty rates worldwide."[19]

Finland's emphasis on women's rights is not new. In rural and agricultural areas, women have traditionally worked alongside men. It was common in the nineteenth century to send girls to school and keep boys at home to work on farms. Women continued to work with men in farming, labor, temperance, and youth movements, and when the country formed its first parliament in 1906, nineteen of its MPs were women. Industrialization—which caused a division of labor based on the sexes in many Western countries—came more slowly to Finland, and when it did, women were already out there working.

Despite these advances, however, Finnish women still earn about 20 percent less than Finnish men. Laws passed in the

As chair of the Bank of Finland, Sirrka Hamalainen is one of many Finnish women to hold high-level positions.

1980s attempted to rectify this. Part of the problem is that women do not always have the higher-paying jobs. There are still very few women senior managers in the top companies, for example, although women are being encouraged to apply for these jobs.

HOUSING

Whether apartments, houses, or cabins, Finnish homes reflect a love of natural materials and simple, elegant design. According to British writer Deborah Swallow:

> Finnish homes can be described as being "Scandinavian" in style. The décor is usually white or cream walls with a few choice pictures and white built-in cupboards with either white or natural wood skirting and architrave. Light-coloured wooden bookshelves, light-colored sofas and chairs and perhaps a leather comfy chair are about the only furniture. Side tables, coffee tables and all the "clutter" of a British home is kept to a minimum.[20]

The Finns do not like wall-to-wall carpeting, preferring instead polished hardwood floors with area rugs. Many Finns,

THE SPIRIT OF THE SAUNA

Look into the warm heart of any Finn or the steamy center of any Finnish home and what one is most likely to see is a sauna. In a country known for its long, cold winters, nothing quite says Finland like the hot sauna. (It is said SOW-na, not SAW-na.)

With about 1.7 million saunas in Finland—one for every three people—just about everybody either owns one or has access to one. Most apartment and office buildings include a sauna. To the Finns, the sauna is necessary for mental, physical, and spiritual health. It is good for sore muscles, aching bones, and sagging spirits. It is a place to relax, reflect, and revive, especially after a long day of work.

Part of the sauna experience is using a birch-tree branch and leaves as whisks to lightly tap and scrape the skin (not flog as some people think). This stimulates circulation and leaves the skin glowing with a pleasant aroma. Many Finns cut their branches in the warmer months and save them in the freezer to use in winter. The sauna usually ends with a plunge into whatever body of water is nearby: a pool, a lake, a river, or the sea.

Although the traditional wood-burning sauna is considered the ultimate experience, most Finns today use saunas heated by electric stoves. By pouring water onto big stones in the stoves, the Finns evoke what to them is the spirit of the sauna: steam, or *loyly.*

The sauna, or steam bath, is not a Finnish invention. It has been enjoyed by other countries and cultures around the world, including the Romans, Turks, Celts, Japanese, and American Indians in their sweat lodges. Most likely, the sauna evolved from an open pit with stones used inside dwellings thousands of years ago. Eventually the sauna became a separate building and was considered sacred, where families celebrated many events. It was where most rural women gave birth up until fifty years ago. It was also used to dry flax, cure meat, smoke sausage, ferment malt, wash laundry, and store vegetables.

By the late 1880s, as Finns migrated to the cities and built homes closer together, the private sauna became less popular. For about seventy years, most Finns used the public saunas. Then, when the invention of metal stoves powered by electricity made it possible to put small saunas inside apartments and homes, the private sauna was revived. The Finns brought back an old tradition, adapted it to their modern lives, and exported the spirit of the sauna to the rest of the world.

even those in modern suburbs, still wash their rugs outdoors in rivers and lakes. Special platforms and railings allow them to stand by the water and hang the rugs.

Most young Finns start out by renting apartments, especially in the cities, and eventually end up buying or building houses in outlying areas. Students, families with children, and pensioners all receive housing allowances. Approximately 70 percent of the population over the age of sixty-five own homes. Rentals and home prices in Helsinki are high.

EDUCATION

With a 99 percent literacy rate, the Finns have made education a main priority since the 1800s when a law required men and women to know how to read and write before they could marry. The Finns consider education the key to prosperity, and they invest more in education than any other industrialized country.

Education is free and is required for all children aged seven and up. It includes three levels: primary, secondary, and university. The primary grades one though six teach Finnish children the basics of language, math, history, the environment, and physical education. Grades seven through nine add religion, geography, arts, chemistry, physics, home economics, and a second language.

Secondary schools are either academic or vocational. The three-year academic schools are similar to American high schools and prepare students to take a national test to qualify for university or technical college. Vocational schools prepare students for about twenty-five different job markets, from forestry to food catering. Students can attend these schools for one or two years to qualify for an entry-level job, or for three or four years to qualify for a supervisory job.

About 58 percent of Finnish students go beyond the secondary level, and about 10 percent receive university degrees. Currently there are about eighty thousand students attending twenty-one universities and three arts academies in Finland. The University of Helsinki is the largest, and, with its twenty-six thousand students, it is one of the largest universities in Europe.

HEALTH AND HEALTH CARE

The same high standards that apply to Finland's educational system also apply to its system of health care. It is mostly free and has helped create a high level of national health and one of the lowest infant mortality rates in the world.

Finns can expect to live about 77.4 years, men 73.7 years and women 81.2 years. They are able to rely on health-care centers throughout the country for most doctor visits. (A few doctors practice individually.) The government runs most of the hospitals at which patients have to pay only 13 percent of any cost. In addition, dental care is provided free for all children up to the age of seventeen.

The Finns take responsibility for their own health and that of their children. About ten years ago, Finland had one of the highest rates of heart disease in the world, caused by a diet of dairy foods and fatty, salty meats and sauces. With the help of an education campaign at schools and medical centers, they were able to reduce the rate considerably, although it is still high compared to other parts of the world. After cardiovascular disease, the leading causes of death in Finland are cancer, accidents, and respiratory and gastrointestinal diseases. Related concerns are growing rates of obesity and type 2 diabetes.

RELIGION

Finland's two official state churches are the Finnish Evangelical Lutheran Church and the Orthodox Church. The majority of Finns (about 85 percent) are Lutherans. Approximately 1 percent, or fifty-five thousand, are Orthodox Catholics. Another 1 percent are Roman Catholics, Jews, or Protestants of other denominations. About 12 percent of Finns have no religious affiliation.

Lutheranism took over from Roman Catholicism as Finland's official state religion in the late 1500s when their first bishop, Michael Agricola, translated parts of the Bible into Finnish. In Finland, religion is taught in school. If at least three students want to study a religion, the school must provide lessons. If students do not want to study religion, they can study philosophy instead.

The Finns consider their religious beliefs to be a private matter. Although most attend church for special occasions such as marriages, baptisms, funerals, and holidays, only about 8 percent attend church regularly. At least half of Finnish churchgoers disagree with some or all of the church's doctrine.

LANGUAGE

Finland's two official languages are Finnish and Swedish. In many parts of the country, billboards and street signs appear in both languages. Only 6 percent of Finland's population speaks Swedish as their first language. Another 1 percent speaks Lappish or Romany. The majority—93 percent—speaks Finnish.

Finnish is a unique language, neither Scandinavian nor European. Unlike Swedish, Norwegian, and Danish, which are Indo-European languages, Finnish is a Finno-Ugric language, originating in northern and central Asia. It is related to Estonian, Hungarian, Lappish, and some Siberian languages.

Words in Finnish are long, with many double vowels and consonants and the addition of suffixes to change meaning. There is no gender, and there are no articles like *a* or *the*. The let-

LIHAVAKALAJÄRVET
BUOIDDESGUOLLEJÁVRRIT

Words in the Finnish language are typically very long. This sign depicts the longest place name in Finland.

ter *v* is sometimes pronounced as a *w*, depending on the surrounding vowels. The first syllable of every word is always stressed, and all vowels are pronounced. In fact, because most of its letters are pronounced, Finnish is one of the easiest languages to write when heard. Linguist Mario Pei called it a clear-cut language: "The clear-cut language gives all its vowels, whether stressed or unstressed, a definite, easily perceptible value. Such tongues as Finnish, Czech, and Italian can be taken down from dictation even if one does not know them thoroughly."[21]

Very few Finnish words have made their way into the English language. Two that have are *sauna,* meaning steam bath, and *tundra,* meaning a flat or slightly hilly, treeless plain with barren topsoil found in arctic and subarctic regions.

FOOD

Finnish food evolved to feed a rural peasant population in a cold climate. Since then, the basic Finnish diet has not changed that much, despite some Swedish, Russian, European, and modern fast-food influences. Staples still include potatoes, turnips, cabbage, rye bread, soups, stews, and various meat and fish dishes, including salmon, herring, trout, liver, reindeer, chicken, beef, and pork. The most popular seasonings are dill and cardamom. One favorite dish is macaroni and ground beef.

The Finns usually eat a small breakfast, and about half the population eats two additional hot meals a day: *lounas* (lunch), the largest meal, at noon, and *paivällinen* (supper) about 5:00 P.M. For special occasions, the Finns lay out a *pitopöytä,* a buffet with soups, salads, salted and pickled fish, cold cuts, bread, cheese, and desserts.

The Finns love dairy products, such as milk and cheese. A popular dessert is *viili,* made of yogurt. They also like meatballs and *makkara* (sausages) and, in the summer, boiled crayfish. Regional specialties include Karelian pies and *kalakukko* fish pies with rye crusts. Mushrooms and berries, which grow everywhere and are available to anyone who wants to pick them, are used often in Finnish cooking. As desserts and sauces, lingonberries (which look like small cranberries) and cloudberries (which look like golden raspberries) are popular. The Finns seldom drink tea, but drink a lot of *kahvi* (coffee). It is served with every meal and often with *pulla,* a wheat bun.

EXTREME FINLAND: THE BEST AND WORST

Writer Seija Sartti compiled a list of what makes Finland such a country of extremes, in addition to its remote location. Comparing Finland to other countries in the EU, she described the ways in which Finland comes out on top or falls to the bottom. Her article appeared in the *Helsingin Sanomat* (June 3, 2003).

In the "best" category, the Finns can boast of the following:

They are the most competitive country in the world, based on a report from the World Economic Forum. They have the largest share of women in the workforce (48 percent of the overall total) and the most literate teenagers. They eat more ice cream and drink more milk per person. They exercise more (80 percent aged fifteen and older do some form of physical exercise at least 3.5 hours per week). They have the greatest density of fishermen and hunters. They have all the flying squirrels in the EU. They are the best paper and newsprint recyclers and also the world's leading consumer of paper. Helsinki is the world's cleanest city, according to one study. Finland has the largest land area north of the Arctic Circle, the smoothest customs procedures, and the least amount of government corruption.

In the "worst" category, the Finns fare as follows:

Finland is the most expensive country in the EU. It is also the most sparsely populated, but the most violent (155 killings, 400 attempted killings, and 1,300 suicides per year). It has the least amount of highways, police, and foreigners (1.9 percent of the population, or about one hundred thousand). Finns are the least likely to want to be self-employed (in one study, 69 percent said they wanted to be employees, compared to 71 percent of Portuguese who said they wanted to run their own businesses). They are the worst sleepers in the EU (up to twice as likely to have sleep disorders), the worst eaters of lamb and mutton (they say "it tastes like wool"), and the biggest cheapskates when it comes to buying clothes. They also drink the strongest coffee and almost as much as the Swedes. This may be why, says Sartti, Finns are the most wired people in the world—and perhaps why they cannot sleep.

Restaurants in Finland offer a variety of cuisines. Italian food is very popular and even small towns have a pizza parlor. On Wednesday nights, restaurants and bars are packed for what the Finns call *pikku viikonloppu,* little weekend.

According to a recent article in the *Helsingin Sanomat,* Finland's young people are developing bad eating habits. Many feel they are too busy to eat regular meals and so snack instead, men usually on pizza and women on candy and soda. The healthiest eaters in Finland are women over fifty-five living in the eastern part of the country where the original peasant diet, high in fiber with rye bread and porridge, still prevails.

DRESS

The Finns are the opposite of flashy, fashion-conscious dressers. In keeping with their reserved nature and their desire to blend in, they dress comfortably and practically. According to business writer Deborah Swallow, "Generally speaking, clothing for the Finns is practical; it's what they use to cover themselves up and keep themselves warm." [22]

They also dress casually, even for work. Although some managers might wear suits and ties, most workers wear more casual outfits, including jeans. Women wear pants more often than dresses. They do not use a lot of makeup or nail polish and prefer simple, well-designed jewelry. Because the Finns do not like to stand out (with a few glamorous or bohemian exceptions), they rarely comment on one another's clothes.

According to Swallow, the Finns like to switch from outdoor to indoor shoes and even take off the indoor shoes:

> In winter most people wear their boots and go to work carrying their indoor shoes in a bag. Open-toed sandals worn with or without socks are always in vogue. One of the things I have noticed is that people often take their shoes off indoors and in public. On the airplane, in training rooms or even in business meetings, shoes will be slipped off, without any self-consciousness. [23]

This down-to-earth attitude captures much of the Finnish character and approach to daily living. Whether living and working in a rural area where they are wired into the high-tech world, or working in a modern office building with a view of the natural world, they are never far from the forest, physically or emotionally.

6

Celebrating Nature in Arts and Entertainment

Just as the natural wilderness of the forest is close to the Finnish people in their daily lives, it also plays an important part in their special celebrations, sporting events, and artistic expression. Finland's forests are the source of both primitive myths and romantic ideals and thus an inspiration for a unique cultural perspective. According to Aarne Reunala, director of the Finnish Forest Research Institute: "Finland's cultural history accommodates barbarism and romance, both a backwoods mentality and a highly evolved culture. Finnish culture has its roots deep in the forests, deeper than any other European culture." [24]

Sports

Summer or winter, the Finns enjoy being outdoors watching or participating in many types of sports. As fans, their favorite sport is ice hockey, with two or three matches a week to watch, culminating in the spring World Championships. In the colder months, they also enjoy watching basketball, volleyball, and track and field. In the summer months, most cities and towns have a soccer team playing in a national league. A new stadium in Helsinki hosts many of these games. Outside the cities, the most popular team sport is *pesäpallo*, a type of baseball. The Finns also love car racing and rallying. Finnish race-car driver Mika Häkkinen, now retired, was a 1998 Formula One Driver's champion.

The Finns do more than just watch sports, however. They are enthusiastic participants, starting early in school, where their physical education is encouraged. In the warmer months, they enjoy hiking, cycling, river rafting, fishing, hunting, and golf. Hunting in Finland is highly regulated, but about three hundred thousand people hunt each fall, more per capita than in any other country in Europe. Golf has become popular. There are now about seventy golf courses throughout the country. During the long summer days it is possible to play past midnight on some courses. Some golfers even play in the winter, using red balls on frozen lakes. Other popular winter sports include skiing, snowmobiling, snowshoeing, ice fishing, dogsledding, and reindeer safaris.

HOLIDAYS AND FESTIVE TRADITIONS

Reflecting the changing seasons, Finland's two most important celebrations are Midsummer's Day in summer and Christmas in winter. The Finns also celebrate May Day and Independence Day.

May Day, or *vappu,* is celebrated on the first of May, to honor students and workers. Traditionally a day of political

Players on Finland's national hockey team celebrate a goal during the 2003 World Championships. Ice hockey is Finland's most popular sport.

marches and speeches, it has been taken over by young people in Finland as a spring festival. On the night before, students place a white student's cap on the head of the mermaid statue in Helsinki harbor and then get an early start on partying.

The Finns welcome the official start of summer—the summer solstice and the longest day of the year—with a holiday called Midsummer's Day, or *juhannus.* It is celebrated on the Saturday between June 20 and June 26. In a gesture going back to ancient pagan rituals, they light bonfires and gather around them with music and dance to ward off evil spirits and celebrate the fertility and light associated with summer.

In contrast, Independence Day, December 6, is quiet and somber. Many Finns put candles in their windows at 6:00 P.M. and visit the graves of war comrades or heroes where they also leave candles. They might also attend a military parade. Most are also glued to their televisions watching the President's Ball. Every year the president invites certain honored citizens as well as government officials. The event has become a media spectacle on a par with the Hollywood Academy Awards.

A Finnish Santa Claus poses with his reindeer in Lapland. Christmas is an extremely important family holiday in Finland.

Christmas is a family holiday in Finland. It is celebrated on Christmas Eve, and the Finns look forward to it all year. On December 1, they put up Advent calendars and candles. The Sunday before Christmas, they buy and decorate a tree, often with small international flags and geometric shapes made with straw. Many visit the graves of loved ones on Christmas Eve where they leave candles and wreaths. Then they return home to enjoy a sauna; to eat special foods, including ham, cod, rice pudding, and Christmas pies; and to welcome Father Christmas (usually a father or neighbor) with gifts. On Christmas Day, families spend a quiet day together and some go to church.

MEDIA

With close to a 100 percent literacy rate, the Finns are avid readers and library users. Close to 4 million Finns (90 percent) read a morning newspaper every day. The main daily newspaper is the *Helsingin Sanomat* (*Helsinki News*).

Finland's three hundred popular magazines cover many areas, from news and general interest to family, home, and hobbies. The most popular magazine is *Aku Ankka* (*Donald Duck*), a weekly comic that has been teaching Finnish children to read for more than fifty years. The only news magazine is *Suomen Kuvalehti.* The largest computer magazine is *Mikro Bitti.*

MUSIC

The Finns enjoy a rich and varied musical landscape, from classical and folk to jazz, pop, and rock. In the warmer months, they take advantage of many beautiful outdoor settings for concerts and festivals. There are about thirteen professional and eighteen semiprofessional orchestras throughout the country, including the Helsinki Philharmonic. Clubs in Helsinki promote a lively jazz and rock scene.

Traditional Finnish folk music is a blend of European and Russian sounds and uses violins, clarinets, accordions, and the kantele, the oldest instrument in Finland. A type of zither, it is flat with from five to forty strings. It can be held and played or placed on a lap or table. One modern group that specializes in this music is Värttinä.

Dominating the classical music scene is Finland's most famous composer, Jean Sibelius (1865–1957). He contributed to the rise of Finnish nationalism in the 1800s when he drew upon ancient Finnish melodies to write his masterpiece, *Finlandia.*

FESTIVE FINLAND

The Finns celebrate their love of music and dance by attending more than seventy festivals a year. They go to see and hear up to twenty thousand performers a year, offering almost every type of music and dance, from chamber and concert music to folk, jazz, rock, and tango. Most of these music festivals are held in the warmest months of June, July, and August, with a few in the spring and the fall.

The most famous and popular is the monthlong Savonlinna Opera Festival held every July in the courtyard of the Olavinlinnia Castle. The castle was built in the Lake District in the 1400s by the Swedish to protect Finland's eastern borders from the Russians. Both the castle itself and the setting—on a small island between two large lakes—provide a dramatic, beautiful backdrop for the festival. For more than ninety years, it has been attracting international opera performers.

Two well-known jazz festivals are held in Espoo outside Helsinki in April and in Pori in July. In the past, the Espoo festival has attracted performers such as Ray Charles, Dave Brubeck, and Nina Simone. The Pori Jazz Festival on the south coast of Finland also attracts international artists and includes up to one hundred different concerts on ten stages.

Also popular are the Tampere Biennale in March, the Midnight Sun Jatajaiset and the Provinssirock in June, the Kaustinen Folk Music Festival in July, and the Tampere International Theatre Festival in August. The Tampere Biennale features new Finnish music and is held in even-numbered years. The Midnight Sun Jatajaiset has been held in Rovaniemi for thirty-one years to celebrate the folk music of Lapland. Also called the International Folklore Festival of Nightless Nights, it is held in a downtown park on the river. Provinssirock in western Finland is a big rock festival where up to sixty different bands perform on five stages. The Kaustinen Folk Music Festival includes folk and rock music. Each year the festival features the music of another country, most recently the folk music of Greece. The Tampere International Theatre Festival features six days and nights of drama, music, and dance for people of all ages. The thirty-five-year-old festival attracts up to thirty different groups from all over Europe and Russia.

His name now graces Finland's most prestigious music academy in Helsinki. Many graduates of this academy have gone on to achieve international fame, such as cellist Seppo Laamanen, pianist Timo Mikkilä and composer Esa-Pekka Salonen (now the conductor of the Los Angeles Philharmonic). The academy also has departments devoted to the study of folk music and jazz.

The UMO Jazz Orchestra is the only professional big band in Finland. It pleased international critics when it played with

Natalie Cole and Manhattan Transfer on their European tours. Finland also has its share of popular and rock singers and groups. Popular performers include rock legend Jussi Raittinen, whose group, Jussi and the Boys, has been performing for thirty years, and Eino Grön, who has been singing songs from tango to folk for more than forty years.

Some well-known rock groups include the Leningrad Cowboys, HIM (love metal), Bomfunk (electro/hip-hop/funk), Waltari and Stratovarius (both heavy metal), and 22 Pistepirkko, whose eccentric pop sound has been described by author Jari Muikku as "Arctic hysteria blends with the winds sweeping the prairies of North America." [25] One heavy metal group called Nightwish uses gloomy melodies and an opera singer as their lead vocalist. Finland also has a surf band—Laika and the Cosmonauts—and several dance/funk/techno groups such as Waldo's People.

Jean Sibelius composes at the piano. Sibelius is Finland's most famous classical composer.

DANCE

Despite their reserved nature, the Finns love to dance, especially ballroom dancing. Many restaurants and hotels hire small orchestras and hold dance evenings where people come to show off their waltzes, foxtrots, and tangos. The tango (which originated in Argentina) was first introduced to the Finns in 1913. Influenced in part by a German marching rhythm, the Finnish version of the tango uses a heavier step than the original. It reached the peak of its popularity in the 1950s and 1960s, when tango dances were held everywhere and tango music was at the top of the music charts. In 1964, it was finally outsold and outranked in Finland by the Beatles.

The Finns nurture classical dance, too. Helsinki's opera company has its own ballet school and there are several dance groups throughout the country. In the summertime, many local bands and singers play on outdoor stages called *lavatanssit* and people dance the rowdy *humppa,* described as a cross between ballroom dancing and an American hoedown.

FILM AND THEATER

Finland produces about twelve movies a year. Subsidized by the government and the television industry, Finland's film industry is small compared to others in Europe. Many of the Finnish filmmakers work with small budgets and cut corners. Although their movies might lack polish, they shine with talent and innovation and are unafraid to tackle difficult subjects.

One popular director is Markku Polonen, who nostalgically explores the Finnish countryside of the 1960s and 1970s in films like *The Land of Happiness, The Last Wedding,* and *A Summer by the River.* His more recent film, *On the Road to Emmaus,* depicts rural life today as people's lives have been uprooted and traditional bonds broken. Other filmmakers like Olli Saarela, Jarmo Lampela, and Auli Mantila explore modern themes about the role of the individual in society, changes in the way people live and work in small towns, and the strength people find within themselves. Documentary filmmakers portray far-ranging topics, from sex-change operations (Ilpo Pohjola's *Plain Truth*) to indigenous people living in the Arctic regions (Markku Lehmuskallio's *Seven Songs from the Tundra*).

Like the film industry, Finland's theaters are also subsidized by the government. In all there are about sixty professional theater groups throughout the country, including those that perform in Swedish, Saami, and Romany. At least

THE BROTHERS KAURISMÄKI

Finland's best-known filmmakers are brothers Mika and Aki Kaurismäki. They began making films together in the early 1980s but eventually broke off into separate paths. Older brother Mika has studied and worked in Russia, Germany, the United States, and, most recently, Brazil. His movies have more of an international, mainstream flavor and often involve crime chases and road trips (*Helsinki Napoli All Night Long, L.A. Without a Map*). His most recent films have been documentaries shot in Brazil, such as *Sounds of Brazil.*

Aki Kaurismäki's films are more intellectual and often capture the tension between reserve and emotion in the Finnish character. His films fall into three categories: adaptation of classics (such as *Crime and Punishment*), improvised odysseys (*Leningrad Cowboys Go America*), and stories of working-class people. His most recent film, *The Man Without a Past,* was awarded the Grand Prix at the Cannes Film Festival in 2002 and was nominated for an Academy Award for Best Foreign Film of 2002.

half of the Finnish people go to the theater once a year. In the summer, they brave rain and mosquitoes to sit in open-air theaters. One of the largest, near Tampere, seats eight hundred people in an area that can be revolved to face different parts of the surrounding performance.

Many Finnish stage productions are based on classics by Shakespeare and Finnish novelists such as Aleksis Kivi (1834–1872) who wrote *Seven Brothers.* Modern playwrights explore themes similar to those of filmmakers and include Jussi Parvinen, Esa Kirkkopelto, Reko Lundan, and Ilpo Tuomarila. Their plays have examined superficial fashion versus a search for meaning, human strength and a better world, turning points in the lives of everyday people, and the follies of the rich and the powerful.

LITERATURE

The first major literature to appear in Finland was a collection of epic tales, songs, poems, and magic charms called the *Kalevala,* published in 1835 and 1849. They were written down by Elias Lönnrot (1802–1884), a country doctor who took time off from practicing medicine to do so. The idea of Finnish nationalism was growing, and he wanted to capture the old rural ways of life before they disappeared. According to translator Francis Magoun Jr.:

One of his chief aims was to create for Finnish posterity a sort of poetical museum of ancient Finno-Karelian peasant life, with its farmers, huntsmen and fishermen, seafarers and sea-robbers, the latter possibly faint echoes from the Viking Age, also housewives, with social and material patterns looking back no doubt centuries—all reflecting a way of life that was, like the songs themselves, already in Lönnrot's day destined for great changes if not outright extinction.[26]

Since those early myths were captured by Lönnrot, the forest has continued to play an important part in Finnish literature. According to Aarne Reunala, director of the Finnish Forest Institute, "Finnish literature has been to a great extent about the forest, describing the tensions between life in the wilderness, daily life in the countryside and urban life."[27]

Finland's forests play a large role in the country's literature, providing the setting and thematic focus for many Finnish novels.

Finland's first great novelist was Aleksis Kivi (1834–1872), whose *Seven Brothers* described the stubbornness and strength of those living in rural areas. Although it was the first novel to be published in Finnish (in 1870), it was not appreciated at the time, and Kivi died in poverty. Gradually the themes in Finnish literature began to include the effects of industrialization, war, and urban living.

Toivo Pekkanen (1902–1957) wrote about the difficulties of working-class life in several novels and memoirs. He is known as the master of the social epic. Novelist and short story writer Juhani Aho (1861–1920) described tensions in the Finnish population set against the beauty of nature.

In 1939, Frans Emil Sillanpää (1888–1964) was awarded the Nobel Prize for Literature. His novels and short stories described rural Finns living with the land in a somewhat idealized way. In the 1940s and 1950s, Mika Waltari (1908–1979) became one of the best known Finnish writers internationally. In addition to historical novels like *The Egyptian*, he wrote mystery novels, short stories, plays, literary criticism, and articles. In the 1940s, Swedish-speaking Tove Jansson (1914–2001) began publishing her children's books about the Moomins, whimsical cartoon trolls who resemble hippos.

Since the 1960s, Finnish literature has reflected more international influences, and at the same time, described personal, family, and social issues. Novelist Kari Hotakainen won the Finlandia Prize for Literature in 2002 for his *Trench Street*, about troubles a man faces while trying to reunite his family and buy a house. Women writers Leena Lander, Anja Kauranen, and Rosa Likson describe the difficulties women face as they try to balance their own needs against the values of society and family relationships. Some modern writers still return to the forest. In Antti Tuuri's book of short stories, *Finland Lives Off Its Forests*, the main character tries to rehabilitate his forest holdings.

The folklore of the forest and the theme of the forest comforting the lonely have greatly influenced Finnish poetry. Early poetry of Johan Runeberg (1804–1877), Eino Leino (1878–1926), and Veikko Koskenniemi (1885–1962) dealt with patriotic, mythical, and classical themes. After the 1950s, Finnish poetry became more experimental, humorous, introspective, and critical of society. Some well-known modern poets include Pentti Saarikoski (1937–1983), Eva-Liisa

Manner (1921–1996), Paavo Haavikko (1931–), and Pentti Saaritsa (1941–). Saarikoski introduced a conversational style and
wrote about people isolated by their ideas. Haavikko, who is
also well known as a publisher and business and television
writer, uses the images of nature in his poetry to describe social
and political issues. Saaritsa, who has published more than
twenty volumes of poetry, is known as a social critic with a
touch of melancholy.

PAINTING, SCULPTURE, AND PHOTOGRAPHY

Although the Finnish people enjoy contemporary art, it is the romantic style of nineteenth-century artists that resonates most
with their love of nature. These artists captured a golden era of
unspoiled forests and country landscapes. The most famous of
these artists was Akseli Gallen-Kallela (1865–1931), whose paintings were inspired by historical myths, including the *Kalevala*.
Another much-loved artist was Albert Edelfelt (1854–1905),
whose paintings of rural life are like photographs. Pekka Halonen (1865–1933) painted winter scenery. The most famous
woman painter of the era, Helene Schjerbeck (1862–1946), was
also the first to move into a style of realism, with self-portraits
that depicted the situation of Finnish women.

During the last four decades in Finland, interest in experimental, abstract modern art has increased and plans have
been under way for a new museum. It finally opened in
Helsinki in 1998. Called Kiasma, it is the most-visited museum
in Finland. Finnish modern art includes a wide variety of
forms, themes, and materials, sometimes combined in the
same piece, and borrowed from other mediums such as
comics, television, and movies. Three young artists who work
in this manner are Janne Kaitala, Jukka Korkeila, and Janne
Räisänen. Marianna Uutinen creates body in her paintings by
dripping or squeezing the paint onto the canvas. Nina Roos
deliberately makes the objects in her paintings blurry as a
comment on how we perceive the world. An older artist, Rafael
Wardi, who has been showing his work since 1947, now works
in pastel and crayon, creating powerful portraits of his wife
who is suffering from Alzheimer's disease.

Three well-known sculptors are Eila Hiltunen, Kain Tapper, and Laila Pullinen. In the 1960s, Hiltunen created a massive tribute to composer Jean Sibelius that took four years to
complete. It weighs twenty-two tons and resembles the pipes

CHAMPIONS OF THE WEIRD AND WACKY

Perhaps almost as much as music and dance, the Finns love a good contest—the funnier and stranger, the better! While some of these far-out festivals (such as cattle calling, ice swimming, beer drinking, jelly doughnut eating, and karaoke) could be held almost anywhere, only in Finland do you find people lining up to sit in saunas or to carry their wives over obstacle courses before passing out.

The Annual Wife-Carrying Contest attracts couples from all over the world every July in Tampere. The first husband to carry his wife across the 760-foot course, leaping over timber and wading through water, wins his wife's weight in beer. The contest is more than one hundred years old and, according to local legend, started when a bully challenged other men to prove their worth by carrying their wives: either their own, a stolen wife, or someone else's. The most recent champions are a couple from Estonia who completed the course in just over a minute.

For the first time, a foreigner also won the women's division of the World Championships in Sauna Sitting. Described as the world's hottest contest, it is held every July in the lakeside town of Heinola north of Helsinki. The most recent winner in the women's division, a thirty-six-year-old woman from Belarus, managed to sit in a sauna cranked up to 230°F (the normal is 175–195°F) for thirteen minutes. The winner in the men's division lasted sixteen minutes and fifteen seconds. The contest attracted eighty contestants from fifteen countries willing to take the heat.

A few other unusual festivals include the World Mosquito-Killing Championship, the Boot-Throwing Championships, the Fishing by Hand Competition, the Anthill Competition, the Poikkinainti Festival, and Sleepyhead Day. The winner of the Anthill Competition is the brave person who can sit the longest on an anthill—naked. The Poikkinainti Festival celebrates cross-border marriages. Held in the border village of Pello on the Torniojoki River between Sweden and Finland, its highlight is a wedding ceremony in the middle of the river. On Sleepyhead Day—July 27—the person chosen as the laziest in the seaside town of Naantali is woken early in the morning and thrown into the sea. This splash is followed by a carnival with music and dance.

of an organ welded together. Today it sits in Sibelius Park in the Töölö district of Helsinki. Tapper's *Rock of Calvary* was the first abstract sculpture to be displayed in a church. Pullinen's *Sun in the Fells* combines copper plates blasted into a plaster mold; she often combines abstract forms with titles from mythology or nature.

Three young modern photographers are Esko Männikkö, Jyrki Parantainen, and Magnus Scharmanoff. Männikkö photographs lonely men living in solitude in remote areas of Finland, portraying them as bohemian antiheroes and as the stereotypical gloomy Finnish men. Recently, he has been photographing similar men in the United States. Parantainen builds detailed room interiors and then photographs them after he has set them on fire and burned them down. Scharmanoff photographs famous works of Finnish art he re-creates as stage sets, often starring himself.

ARCHITECTURE

Finland has its own unique architectural style: a combination of European and Russian influences with modern designs and natural materials. According to Aarne Reunala, "Finland developed an original 'forest style' in which international trends were blended with the Finnish." [28]

Finland's most famous architect was Alvar Aalto (1898–1976). He was also an urban planner, an interior designer, an industrial designer, and a furniture designer. From the 1930s on, he helped introduce the style of functionalism, meaning the form of something (a building, a chair) should follow its function. In all, he designed two hundred buildings and three city centers. His projects in Finland included the Finlandia House in 1971, a conference hall next to Parliament, and the layout of the city of Rovaniemi in Lapland. Using natural woods and open space, he liked to create a feeling of luxury without ostentation. His ideas and designs continue to influence Finnish architects today.

Mikko Heikkinen and Markku Komonen have incorporated the elements of nature into their buildings such as the Finnish Science Center and the Rovaniemi airport. The science center uses geometrical shapes, wire-supported canopies, and bridges to portray a feeling of defying gravity and reaching outdoors and into the universe. The airport also uses canopies and has an opening in the roof where the sun comes through and shines on the floor, moving every day to reflect the earth's orbit.

Pekka Helin and Tuomo Siitonen have designed a training center for the Finnish Metalworkers Union. Surrounded by pine trees and rock formations on a lake, it includes several buildings designed to follow and blend in with the natural terrain. One of their most recent office buildings is the Nokia headquarters in Helsinki. Inside, large open areas are softened by wood. Outside, the steel and glass reflect the sky and the sea.

Whether inside or outside, the Finns are able to enjoy and celebrate their love of the natural world. This can be seen in so many areas reflecting their lives, from sports and entertainment to literature, painting, and architecture.

Maintaining Balance in the Twenty-first Century

Even though the Finns are still at the top of the world, with one of the highest standards of living, they face many challenges in the coming years. Basically, they are learning to balance priorities in the areas of environment, immigration, and globalization. Specifically, this means preserving natural beauty without sacrificing economic and recreational uses, maintaining a cohesive society while accepting immigrants from other cultures, and retaining and sharing the best parts of their own unique culture as they move into the global economy and international politics.

Balancing Environmental Issues

According to a 2002 study conducted by Yale and Columbia Universities, Finland is the most environmentally healthy country in the world. According to an article on a government Web site, Finland was ranked number one out of 142 nations in another survey when it came to taking care of the environment. Yet, according to an earlier study and various environmentalist groups, Finland's ancient forests are being destroyed, its lakes are among the most polluted in Europe, and its seas are suffering from a variety of ailments, from lack of oxygen to the danger of oil spills. In reality, the truth is most likely in between the rosy picture painted by the government and the bleak future predicted by environmentalist groups. There are environmental problems that need to be solved. Like many countries in the world, Finland has become aware that today's industrial development can threaten tomorrow's natural resources if not planned carefully. The Finnish government has embraced the concept of sustainable development: development that meets the needs of the present without compromising the ability of future generations to meet their own needs.

Many Finns, like this logger, depend on the forests for their livelihoods. The Finnish government has established guidelines to reconcile timber production with environmental protection.

Although not a new concept, it was first defined on an international level in 1987 and has been evolving ever since and is easily understood by the Finnish people, with their love of nature and respect for the environment. Everyone in Finland has free access to the wilderness, including the right to pick mushrooms and berries on privately owned land.

FINLAND'S FORESTS

The idea of balancing current and future needs is especially applicable to Finland's forests. Covering more than 70 percent of the land, they are the country's main natural resource and the main topic of environmental debate. According to travel writers Jennifer Brewer and Markus Lehtipuu, "In Finland, forestry products are the main source of income and employment, the main cause of pollution and the main topic of environmental debate." [29]

Finland has been managing its forests since the timber industry began developing in the nineteenth century. In 1886 a law was passed in Finland prohibiting the wasteful use of forests. By the 1960s, the idea that forests can be cultivated specifically for harvesting took over. Today, about 80 percent of Finland's forests are privately owned and cultivated and the rest are protected by the Finnish Forest and Park Service. According to Aarne Reunala, director of the Finnish Forest Research Institute, "At present, scarcely any country has a more effective organization of support and advice for forest-owners than Finland." Recently, the government's Forest 2000 Programme set down new guidelines to "reconcile timber production with protection of the environment and the use of the forests for recreational purposes." [30]

According to Reunala, reconciling these various needs will continue to be a difficult challenge. Several environmental research and activist groups, such as Greenpeace, think that private citizens and the government should be doing more to prevent the destruction of "ancient" or "old-growth" forests, those with natural diversity. As more of these are being replaced with just one or two commercial species, the biodiversity of the forests and surrounding plants and animals is being threatened. The Finnish minister of the environment disputes this claim.

WATER AND AIR POLLUTION

The by-products of the forestry industry contribute to water and air pollution. According to Brewer and Lehtipuu,

> Paper and pulp industries provide work for thousands, but also cause environmental hazards, which are easily seen in areas surrounding factories. To put it bluntly,

RULES AND MORE RULES

According to travel writers Jennifer Brewer and Markus Lehtipuu, the Finns follow a lot of rules and have a lot of rules to follow. As they describe in the Lonely Planet's guidebook *Finland:*

> Finns are either the world's worst bureaucrats or the world's most obedient people, judging by the plethora of rigorously enforced rules and regulations that govern Finnish life.

> Road laws in particular are strictly enforced. The government collects hundreds of millions of markka annually as income from traffic tickets alone. . . .

> A businessperson recently started a small guesthouse offering catering services. If only it was so simple . . . no less than 15 different authorities inspected the building, checking everything from hygiene to plumbing, making sure all rules and every word of the law was obeyed. "In Italy only 50% of EU rules are honoured," remarked the owner of the establishment. "Finland . . . [at that time not an EU member] already obeys 120% of all EU rules!"

> Perhaps the new millennium will bring change now that Finns are showing signs of obedience fatigue. On the other hand, they've always excelled at endurance sports.

pulp factories stink, literally and figuratively. . . . Pulp industries—and other heavy industries long a staple of the Finnish economy—contribute to massive domestic water pollution. . . . Finland, the land of lake, river and ocean, may look idyllic and pristine—but in fact it isn't, or at least not very. A 1997 survey ranked Finland's lake and ocean waters as some of the most polluted in the EU. [31]

According to government reports, however, the levels of pollution have decreased significantly in recent years. In late 2002, the World Water Council ranked Finland number one out of 147 countries it surveyed about access to and use of water.

The Finns are also working on ways to decrease air pollution. With few natural energy resources, they have had to rely in part on wood and coal burning. In keeping with the Kyoto Protocol, they must use other sources of energy. Currently the Finns are planning to add a fifth nuclear reactor, decrease coal burning, and replace old diesel engines, which will greatly reduce emissions. They are also planning to build a permanent nuclear-waste storage facility, which will be operating by 2020.

Although some environmental groups oppose the use of nuclear energy in Finland, others see it as a realistic compromise. According to engineering writer Steve Blankinship:

> As a people and as a country, Finnish concern for the environment is well documented and second to none. But Finland is also a nation of realists. Leaders know the nation must have energy and know that a diverse, well-balanced generation portfolio is the way to assure a reliable, affordable, secure supply of it. [32]

THE BUSY BALTIC

The two arms of the Baltic Sea that reach around Finland—the Gulf of Finland in the south and the Gulf of Bothnia on the west—are also increasingly at risk. They are shallow bodies of water with delicate ecosystems. Various studies conducted by marine biologists have found that in certain parts of the gulfs, there is little or no life at the bottom due to oxygen deprivation. In other parts, invasive species have taken over. Toxic runoff from industrial waste also makes the Baltic one of the most polluted seas in the world. In the past two decades, the cod population has decreased 75 percent, seriously affecting the cod

fishing industry. Finland's own Baltic Sea Protection Program is trying to reduce emissions by half in the next ten to fifteen years. Scientists are continuing to study these problems and their possible impact on economic and human health.

A ship sails out of port in the Gulf of Finland. A heavy volume of maritime traffic in the gulf has threatened the area's ecosystems.

A growing threat to this already fragile environment is the increase in shipping traffic and the possibility of oil dumping and spills, especially in the Gulf of Finland. The gulf has become an important shipping route for Russia. Russia's new, expanding economy is based on oil exports. The Russians are building more oil terminals at the eastern end of the gulf as well as transporting the oil by ship through the Baltic to Germany and other European countries. In 2004, shipping traffic will increase when several more countries fronting the Baltic (Estonia, Latvia, Lithuania, and Poland) join the EU.

Many countries that send ships through the Baltic, including Russia, do not adhere to high safety standards. Their ships, for example, are single hulled and more prone to accidental spilling if hit or stuck in ice. Some ships—up to seventy-five in 2002—deliberately dump their oil. Those resorting to illegal dumping are hard to catch and prosecute. Several Baltic countries, including Finland, are working together to develop standards that make it easier to monitor and catch these ships and prove their violations. They are also pressuring the EU to demand that Russia use safer tankers and increased safety standards in its ports. Greenpeace is demanding that even more-stringent regulations be adopted to ensure safe and environmentally sound shipping. These include the issuing of a Baltic driver's license by an organization like the International Maritime Organization that would require shippers to meet safety standards, follow traffic rules, and be held accountable for illegal dumping.

BALANCING IMMIGRATION ISSUES

Up until the last decade, Finland has been a closed, homogeneous country, with few foreigners. Most Finns and Lapps are descended from the same tribes of people who moved into the area one or two thousand years ago. Even the minority groups—the Swedes and Gypsies—have been in Finland for hundreds of years.

Limited by a strict immigration policy, very few foreigners have been allowed to settle permanently in Finland. Most have been visitors, such as students or temporary workers. In fact, up until about thirty years ago, Finland's population was declining as more people left the country than came in.

Since 1990, Finland has welcomed thousands of Russians like these and other immigrants from former Soviet-controlled countries.

This has changed rapidly in the last ten years. Since 1990, the number of foreigners in Finland has grown from about twenty-one thousand to more than one hundred thousand, a greater increase than in any western European country.

Most of these have been from Russia and its former satellite countries such as Estonia. After the breakup of the Soviet Union in the early 1990s, twenty-two thousand Russians of Finnish descent living in the St. Petersburg area were allowed to settle permanently in Finland as "returning migrants." Others have been refugees from Somalia, Vietnam, and the former Yugoslavia. In all, there are now about 150 different nationalities living in Finland. In just a short period of time, the Finnish people are being forced to change into a more open, multicultural society. This change is taking place at all levels, from personal attitudes to government policies, as Finns weigh the pros and cons of accepting new people.

In general, according to one survey of Finnish authorities, police, border guards, and people in rural areas have a more negative attitude toward immigrants, fearing they will increase unemployment, crime, and disease and interfere with a cohesive social order. On the other hand, teachers and social workers have a more positive attitude toward immigrants, seeing them as an economic resource and source of cultural enrichment.

Most Finnish immigrants live in and around cosmopolitan Helsinki, but they still face a great deal of discrimination, especially in the job market. Their unemployment rate—at 30 percent—is about three times as high as the national average. The jobs they do get tend to be low paying, such as housecleaners and taxi drivers. This situation has several causes: employer prejudice, lack of language skills, lack of verifiable training or college education, and emotional problems caused by war and displacement.

How much help to give these foreigners and how much to expect them to assimilate into Finnish culture are just two of the immigration issues currently facing the Finnish people. According to an article in the *Journal of Ethnic and Migration Studies,* Finnish authorities say they want a pluralistic society, but in reality they expect foreigners to blend in, with no special treatment. To some extent, the values of the welfare state—that support is given equally to everyone—reinforces the idea of blending in, of being the same. However, in May 1999, the Act on the Integration of Immigrants and Reception of Asylum Seekers was passed to help immigrants integrate into Finnish society. It includes specific plans for helping foreign adults and children in several ways, including learning the language, getting job training, or getting started in school. Even so, new arrivals still face discrimination and, in the case of those from Asian and African countries, racism. Although the government is promoting multicultural acceptance, private attitudes and practices are slower to change.

Many Finns realize that their economy will require more workers in the coming years. Finland's population is aging, baby boomers are retiring, and there soon will be more jobs than workers. According to Olavi Koivukangas, a director at the Finnish Institute of Migration, the Finns will have to change their attitude of seeing immigrants as a threat and competition in the labor market and instead see them as an asset: "The Finnish society and attitudes will have to adjust to the temporary and permanent presence of an increasing number of people with foreign background. Immigrants and their children will be a great asset to Finland in the future."[33]

But, how many more immigrants should Finland admit and what criteria should be used in selecting them? Some Finns think too many immigrants are being allowed into their country, and others think too few are. Some researchers and analysts think that potential immigrants should be selected according to the needs of the labor market, based on their education, language, and job skills. Others think that an immigrant's country of origin should be considered.

Compared to other European countries, Finland's rate of immigration is still low but it is expected to increase, especially when ten new countries join the EU in 2004. According to Koivukangas, the Finnish government needs to prepare itself by working out a comprehensive population and migration policy in cooperation with the EU.

BALANCING INTERNATIONAL ISSUES IN THE EURO AGE

Today, Finland's challenges of balancing environmental and immigration priorities are no longer just an internal matter. As a member of the EU since 1995, Finland must now consider these and related issues in an international light. How to accomplish this without sacrificing its own strength and identity is perhaps an even bigger challenge. According to British political scientist David Arter, "A crucial scenario in the twenty-first century may well involve striking the right balance between Finland's inevitably greater commitments on the international stage and the protection and promotion

THE EURO

After 140 years in circulation, the Finnish markka is no longer crossing palms. Along with the people in eleven other EU countries, the Finns have handed over their old currency for the new euro. Worth about $0.8889 in exchange for an American dollar in 2003, the euro is distributed in seven denominations of banknotes and eight denominations of coins. The number of denominations was agreed upon after counting the number from each participating country and figuring out the average.

The seven banknotes are 5 euro, 10 euro, 20 euro, 50 euro, 100 euro, 200 euro, and 500 euro. Each denomination is a different size and color and features a different period of European architecture, from classical to modern. The front of the bill features windows or arches, and the back depicts bridges and a map of Europe. In addition, all bills include the European flag, the initials of the European Central Bank (ECB), the signature of the ECB president, the name *euro* in both Latin and Greek script, and the twelve stars of the EU. The banknotes are the same for all twelve countries. The only thing distinguishing them is the first letter of a code on the back of each bill. Finland's is the letter *L.*

Unlike the euro banknotes, the coins are different for each country. All euro coins have a common front side, but a unique national design on the back side. The euro is divided into one hundred cents. The coins include a 1 cent (E 0.01), a 2 cent, a 5 cent, 10 cent, 20 cent, 50 cent, 1 euro, and 2 euro. The common front side of each euro coin shows the amount, the twelve stars, and a map of Europe.

The back of Finland's euro coins are all the same except for the two largest. They show the year and the heraldic lion that appeared on the markka. The back of Finland's 1-euro coin shows two swans flying over a Finnish landscape, and the back of the 2-euro coin shows the fruit and flowers of the cloudberry.

The euro currency can be used in any of the twelve participating countries, which are Finland, Belgium, Germany, Greece, Spain, France, Ireland, Italy, Luxembourg, the Netherlands, Austria, and Portugal.

In 2002 Finland abandoned use of the Finnish markka as currency and began using the Euro (pictured).

of the indigenous language[s] and cultural traditions that invest a state with its quality as a nation."[34]

When Arter made that observation in the late 1980s, Finland had not yet joined the EU. The Finns were still deciding whether or not the advantages of joining would outweigh the disadvan-

THE EUROPEAN FLAG

The same twelve stars that appear on the euro banknotes and coins also appear on the European flag. With twelve gold stars in a circle on a blue background, the flag represents Europe as a whole, but it also represents the history of the EU and the organizations that led to its formation.

The European flag is actually controlled by three organizations: the Council of Europe, the European Community, and the EU. It was originally designed in Ireland and adopted in 1955 by the Council of Europe to symbolize European unity. The Council of Europe was formed in 1949 as a way to bring Europe together after World War II.

By 1957, a second organization to foster economic growth was established: the EEC. With six members (Belgium, France, Germany, Italy, Luxembourg, and the Netherlands), it evolved into the European Community in ten years with the addition of large energy companies.

By 1986, six more countries had joined the European Community: the United Kingdom, Ireland, Denmark, Greece, Portugal, and Spain. With these twelve member countries, the European Community also adopted the flag with twelve stars, with permission from the Council of Europe.

In 1993 the EU was formed to bring together a single European market with the twelve members of the European Community. It, too, adopted the twelve-star flag. Three years later, when three more countries joined the EU—Finland, Sweden, and Austria—the EU decided to retain the twelve-star design.

A woman sews stars on the European flag. Finland became a part of the united European Community in 1996.

tages. The EU had been evolving since the 1950s as a way to unite and promote European countries economically, politically, and socially. By the time Finland, Sweden, and Austria joined, a total of fifteen countries were working together to establish common policies in many areas, from trade and agriculture to education, energy, and environment. In 2002, twelve EU members, including Finland, began using the same currency: the euro.

Finland was welcomed into the EU as a model country. No longer under Russia's shadow, Finland was seen as a politically and economically strong country with much to contribute. While this has turned out to be true in some ways, the Finns are still forming their own opinions and policies about their new global role in the "Euro Age."

In Finland, just like in Sweden, there is less popular support for EU participation than in other European countries. But those who favor the EU think it has helped Finland in several ways. It has opened up new markets, increased exports and stability, lowered prices, increased selection of consumer goods, and made it easier to do business with one currency. Several mergers between Finnish and Swedish companies have benefited the economy. Membership in the EU has helped make Finland a more visible country, one with important values to share, especially in the areas of human rights and social justice.

Those who question the benefits of belonging to the EU think there is too much competition and that the EU's cutting back agricultural subsidies has harmed farmers too much. Finnish farmers complain about an increase in inspections and bureaucratic paperwork. Most important, the Finns do not want to see the EU compromise what has made their country unique and their right to determine their own course. This is particularly true in the areas of government by consensus and the policy of neutrality.

Currently, the political structure of the EU is evolving, causing further debate between and within countries. It is currently governed by a European Commission, a Council of Ministers, and a European Parliament. The commission is the main administrative body. Currently it has twenty members, two from each of the five largest countries and one from the other ten. The commissioners are appointed by their respective governments and serve four-year terms.

The commission's president is the EU's head of government. Representing the interests of the EU first, the commission supersedes national interests. The Council of Ministers, on the other hand, represents the interests of each country. Each country has one minister, usually the foreign minister. The presidency is a six-month term and rotates among the members. The European Parliament is the democratic public forum, with more than six hundred members elected by popular vote. Its purpose is to question and debate issues and to counterbalance the powers of the commission and the council.

Some members of the EU would like the structure to remain the same—a loose, voluntary affiliation of states—and others would like to see a stronger, more binding union and government, similar to the states and the federal government of the United States. This would include a president with stronger powers, only ten commissioners, and the limiting of seats in the parliament. Currently, some in Finland oppose this idea and consider it undemocratic, while others favor the idea of a stronger president in exchange for a commissioner's post. Used to compromising in coalition governments, the Finns realize that sacrificing some of their autonomy might be beneficial if things run more efficiently.

Another area of debate in the EU and in Finland is the formation of a defense core, an alliance being pushed by France and Germany to increase security. With its policy of military neutrality, Finland has been questioning the purpose of such a group. Some see it as unnecessary competition for NATO, which Finland does not belong to, and others see it as a way of being pushed into NATO. Some favor joining but want it to be open to all members.

These issues—about the structure of the EU, the balance of power among its member nations, and the part Finland will play—will be debated for many years. Just as the Finns are learning to balance environmental and immigration priorities, they are also seeking a comfortable yet vibrant place in the world. They are already well on their way.

FACTS ABOUT FINLAND

GENERAL INFORMATION

Official name: Republic of Finland

Type of government: republic with unicameral parliament (Eduskunta), two hundred members elected by popular vote on a proportional basis to serve four-year terms

Chief of state: president, elected by popular vote for six-year term

Head of government: prime minister, selected by president from majority party after parliamentary elections

Capital: Helsinki

Major cities: Espoo, Tampere, Vantaa, Turku

Official languages: Finnish, Swedish

Other languages: Lappish, Russian

Monetary unit: euro

Exchange rate (2003): $1 U.S. = 0.8889 euro

PEOPLE

Population (2002): 5.2 million

Population growth rate (2002): 0.14%

Density: persons per square mile (2002): 16

Population distribution (2002): urban, 60%; rural, 40%

Population by age (2003): under 15, 17.8%; 15–64, 66.9 %; 65 and over, 15.3 %

Ethnic composition: Finn, 93%; Swede, Lapp, Gypsy, 6%; other, 1%

Religious affiliation: Evangelical Lutheran, 84.6%; Greek Orthodox, 1%; other, 1%; no affiliation, 13.1%

VITAL STATISTICS

Birthrate per 1,000 population (2002): 10.7

Death rate per 1,000 population (2002): 9.5

Infant mortality rate per 1,000 live births (2002): 3.76

Total fertility rate (average births per childbearing woman) (2002): 1.7

Life expectancy at birth (2001): 77.75; males, 74.6; females, 81.5

SOCIAL INDICATORS

Literacy, age 15 and over (2002): total population, 99%

Political participation: eligible voters participating in last national election (2003): 69.7%. Everyone 18 and older has the right to vote.

Working life (2002): labor force, 2.6 million; public services, 32%; industry, 22%; commerce, 14%; finance, insurance, and business services, 10%; agriculture and forestry, 8%; transportation and communications, 8%; construction, 6%; unemployed, 9.1%

ECONOMY

Gross domestic product (2002): $136.2 billion, $26,200 per capita

Annual growth rate (2002): 1.1%

Budget revenue (2000): $36.1 billion

Expenditures (2000): $31 billion

Inflation rate (2002): 1.9% per year

Major export destinations: EU, 58%; United States, 8%

Exports (2001): $40.1 billion (machinery and equipment, chemicals, metals, timber, paper, pulp)

Major import sources: EU, United States

NOTES

CHAPTER 1: AT THE TOP OF THE WORLD

1. Fred Singleton, *A Short History of Finland.* Cambridge, England: Cambridge University Press, 1989, p. 70.

2. Singleton, *A Short History of Finland,* p. 71.

3. Jennifer Brewer and Markus Lehtipuu, *Finland.* Hawthorn, Australia: Lonely Planet, 1999, p. 351.

4. Eeva-Liisa Hallanaro, "Nature in Finland," Virtual Finland, September 2002. http://virtual.finland.fi.

CHAPTER 2: FROM NOMADS AND VIKINGS TO KINGS AND CZARS

5. W.R. Mead, "Perceptions of Finland," in *Finland: People, Nation, State,* Max Engman and David Kirby, eds. London: Hurst, 1989, p. 5.

6. Brewer and Lehtipuu, *Finland,* p. 18.

CHAPTER 3: FROM FARM AND FOREST TO URBAN HIGH TECH

7. Pasi Kuoppamäki, A Web History of Finland, 2000. http://ky.hkkk.fi.

8. Singleton, *A Short History of Finland,* p. 161.

CHAPTER 4: HIGH IDEALS ON SOLID GROUND

9. Singleton, *A Short History of Finland,* p. 154.

10. Joe Brady, "Finland Number One in 2003 World IT Report," Virtual Finland, February 2003.

11. Mead, "Perceptions of Finland," p. 12.

12. Brewer and Lehtipuu, *Finland,* p. 94.

13. Quoted in Mead, "Perceptions of Finland," p. 15.

14. Singleton, *A Short History of Finland,* p. 167.

15. Jukka Nevakivi, "Independent Finland Between East and West," in *Finland: People, Nation, State,* p. 143.

16. Mead, "Perceptions of Finland," p. 13.

CHAPTER 5: NEVER FAR FROM THE FOREST

17. Aarne Reunala, "The Forest and the Finns," in *Finland: People, Nation, State,* p. 55.

18. Brewer and Lehtipuu, *Finland,* p. 33.

19. Karen Christopher, "Family-Friendly Europe," *American Prospect,* April 8, 2002. www.prospect.org.

20. Deborah Swallow, *Culture Shock: A Guide to Customs and Etiquette: Finland.* Portland, OR: Graphic Arts Center, 2001, p. 97.

21. Mario Pei, *The Story of Language.* New York: Meridian Books, 1984, p. 204.

22. Swallow, *Culture Shock,* p. 75.

23. Swallow, *Culture Shock,* p. 77.

CHAPTER 6: CELEBRATING NATURE IN ARTS AND ENTERTAINMENT

24. Aarne Reunala, "Forests and Finnish Culture," Virtual Finland, 2002. http://virtual.finland.fi.

25. Jari Muikku, "Folk, Jazz, and Rock Music in Finland," Virtual Finland, 2000. http://virtual.finland.fi.

26. Elias Lönnrot, *The Kalevala,* trans. Francis Magoun Jr. Cambridge, MA: Harvard University Press, 1963, p. xiv.

27. Reunala, "The Forest and the Finns," p. 53.

28. Reunala, "The Forest and the Finns," p. 53.

CHAPTER 7: MAINTAINING BALANCE IN THE TWENTY-FIRST CENTURY

29. Brewer and Lehtipuu, *Finland,* p. 22.

30. Reunala, "The Forest and the Finns," p. 50.

31. Brewer and Lehtipuu, *Finland,* pp. 22–23.

32. Steve Blankinship, "Big Lessons for a Small Country," *Power Engineering,* April 2003, p. 5.

33. Olavi Koivukangas, "European Immigration and Integration in Finland," Institute of Immigration, February 2003. www.utu.fi.

34. David Arter, "Finland: A Typical Post-Industrial State," in *Finland: People, Nation, State,* p. 243.

GLOSSARY

Arctic Circle: The latitude of 66.5 degrees above the equator that circles the earth and includes the earth's northern frigid zone.

Eduskunta: Finland's parliament, a one-house legislative body with two hundred members.

Finlandization: Foreign policy of neutrality that made a non-Communist country susceptible to the influence of the Soviet Union before the end of the Cold War.

Finno-Ugric: People originating from northern and eastern Europe and northwestern Siberia speaking related languages, including the Finnish, Estonians, Hungarians, and Lapps; subfamily of Uralic family of languages.

joki: A river.

juhannus: Midsummer, the longest day of the year, celebrated at the end of June on Friday evening and Saturday.

Kalevala: The national epic of Finland, which includes poetry, songs, and folktales.

kantele: A traditional stringed instrument similar to a zither. A type of harp, it consists of a flat box with from five to forty strings.

Lappi or Lapland: The province of Finland north of the Arctic Circle.

makkara: Sausage.

Nordic: People or countries of northern Europe, including Finland, Norway, Sweden, Denmark, and Iceland.

Oy: Abbreviation for Osakeyhtiö, used after company names, as in the American *Corp.* for *Corporation* or the British *Ltd.* for *Limited.*

Oyj: Used after company names to signify a group or parent company or owner of several companies or corporations.

pesäpallo: A type of baseball.

pitopöytä: A large buffet table.

revontulet: Northern lights, or aurora borealis. Dancing colored lights that appear in the sky in the earth's northern hemisphere.

Saami: Native people of Finland, known also as Lapps.

sauna: A steam bath in which steam is provided by water thrown on hot stones.

Scandinavia: Peninsula in northern Europe occupied by Norway and Sweden. Another definition includes Denmark, Norway, Sweden, and sometimes Iceland, the Faroe Islands, and Finland.

sisu: Courage, determination, pride, strength of character. Considered a major part of the Finnish makeup.

Suomi: The Finnish name for Finland.

tundra: A flat or slightly hilly, treeless plain found in arctic and subarctic regions such as Lapland. The topsoil is mucky, with a permanently frozen subsoil.

vappu: May Day, or May 1.

CHRONOLOGY

10,000–1800 B.C.
Nomadic tribes arrive in Finland, most likely from the Ural Mountains in western Siberia.

1800–500 B.C.
More tribes of people arrive, some through central Europe.

500 B.C.–A.D. 500
Trade and farming increase as people organize into villages during this period called the Iron Age. Separate tribes emerge in different parts of Finland, and the earliest inhabitants, the Saami, retreat farther north.

800–1000
Vikings from Sweden build fortresses and trading ports on the Aland Islands and parts of southern Finland and the eastern Baltic.

1100–1400
Sweden sends military and religious crusaders into Finland and by 1362 makes Finland a province of Sweden.

1229
City of Turku founded on west coast.

1539
Bishop of Turku, Michael Agricola, translates the Bible's New Testament into Finnish, thus establishing Finnish as a written language for the first time.

1550
The city of Helsinki is established on the south coast as a trading post.

1700–1721
Swedes cede province of Vyborg to Russia after the Great Northern War in which they fought Russia, Denmark, and Poland. Russia destroys much of Finland, and a plague wipes out two-thirds of the population of Helsinki.

1809
Russia takes over all of Finland from Sweden. Finland becomes a partly self-ruling grand duchy under Czar Alexander I.

1812
Russia moves the capital of the Finnish grand duchy from Turku to Helskini so that it is closer to St. Petersburg.

1906
Finns establish their own parliament and give everyone, including women, the right to vote.

1917
Finland declares independence from Russia on December 6, after Russian Republic collapses in revolution. Civil war between Communists (Red Guards) and non-Communists (White Guards) breaks out in Finland for control of the government. After six months of fighting, the White Guards win.

1919
Finland adopts its first constitution and a law professor, Kaarlo Juho Stahlberg, as its first president.

1939–1940
Soviet Russia attacks Finland and takes western Karelia in the Winter War.

1941–1944
Soviet Russia defeats Finland in the Continuation War. German forces, who had been helping the Finnish, are ordered to leave and destroy much of Lapland as they retreat.

1944
Finland makes a peace agreement with the Allies and establishes a policy of international neutrality.

1952
Helsinki hosts the Summer Olympics.

1955
Finland joins the Nordic Council and the United Nations.

1956–1981
Soviet Russia returns Porkkala peninsula, which they had taken as part of peace agreement. Urho Kekkonen becomes Finland's longest-serving president, helping Finland stay neutral during the Cold War.

1973

Finland signs a free trade agreement with the EEC, a fore-runner of the EU.

1975

Finland hosts the Conference on Security and Cooperation in Helsinki.

1995

Finland joins the EU.

2002

Finland elects its first woman president, Tarja Halonen.

2003

Finland's first woman prime minister, Anneli Jäätteenmäki, is selected to lead the government after the parliamentary elections. After four months in office, she resigns after allegations she used confidential foreign policy documents during her campaign. Parliament selects Matti Vanhanen as the new prime minister. Representing the Centre Party, he forms a coalition government among the Centre Party, the Social Democratic Party, and the Swedish People's Party.

For Further Reading

Books

Nonfiction

Finland ... in Pictures. Minneapolis: Lerner, 1991. Basic information about the country with many interesting pictures.

Martin Hintz, *Enchantment of the World: Finland.* Chicago: Children's Press, 1983. Basic information about Finland. Well illustrated, but somewhat dated.

Sylvia McNair, *Finland.* New York: Children's Press, 1997. A nicely illustrated and well-written introduction to Finnish geography, culture, and customs.

Fiction

Toivo Pekkanen, *My Childhood.* Madison: University of Wisconsin Press, 1966. A memoir of growing up in southeast Finland in the early 1900s by one of Finland's major novelists.

Frans Eemil Sillanpää, *People in the Summer Night.* Madison: University of Wisconsin Press, 1966. A novel originally published in 1934. Sillanpää won the Nobel Prize for Literature in 1939.

Web Sites

City of Helsinki (www.hel.fi). Maintained by the city of Helsinki. Includes a good selection of information, including services, events, public services, transportation, and maps. Also includes a virtual tour of the city.

Embassy of Finland (www.finland.org). The site of the Finnish Embassy in Washington, D.C. Includes links to many other sites and pictures of the embassy building, which has won praise for its beautiful Finnish design since it opened in 1994.

The Finnish Institute of International Affairs (www.upi-fiia.fi). Maintained by a private research institute to help the Finns understand international issues, especially in relationship to Finland.

Moominvalley (www.tampere.fi). An exhibit of about one thousand illustrations and sketches of Tove Jansson's Moomin family. Maintained by the Tampere Art Museum, the site also contains information about the author, who died in 2001, and her books.

Sibelius Academy (www.siba.fi). Links to Web sites for many types of Finnish music, including pop, folk, blues, and jazz. Run by the only music university in Finland.

WORKS CONSULTED

BOOKS

Jennifer Brewer and Markus Lehtipuu, *Finland*. Hawthorn, Australia: Lonely Planet, 1999. An informative guidebook for the traveler. Includes sections on history and culture and extensive maps and descriptions of the major areas of the country.

Richard Dauenhauer and Philip Binham, eds., *Snow in May: An Anthology of Finnish Writing, 1945–1972*. Cranbury, NJ: Associated University Presses, 1978. A generous sampling of Finnish literature, including critical essays, poetry, short stories, and plays. Does not include work from the last thirty years.

Jared Diamond, *Guns, Germs, and Steel: The Fates of Human Societies*. New York: W.W. Norton, 1999. Addresses the question of why history developed differently in different parts of the world. Includes information on early reindeer hunters in the area that is now Finland. Winner of the Pulitzer Prize and highly readable.

Max Engman and David Kirby, eds., *Finland: People, Nation, State*. London, England: Hurst, 1989. A collection of essays written by university professors and other scholars originally published in Finland to mark the country's seventieth anniversary of independence.

The Green Guide: Scandinavia/Finland. Watford, England: Michelin Travel, 2001. A beautifully illustrated travel guide to Finland, Norway, Sweden, and Denmark.

Aili Järvenpää, trans., *Salt of Pleasure: Twentieth-Century Finnish Poetry*. St. Paul, MN: New Rivers Press, 1983. Includes the poetry of twenty-six Finnish poets up to the early 1980s.

The Kalevala, Elias Lönnrot. Trans. Francis Magoun Jr. Cambridge, MA: Harvard University Press, 1963. A collection of traditional Finnish songs and lyrics compiled by a country doctor, Elias Lönnrot, and first published in 1835.

George Maude, *Historical Dictionary of Finland.* Lanham, MD: Scarecrow Press, 1995. An alphabetical listing of important people, events, and ideas in Finland's history. Clearly written and easy to use, with an extensive bibliography.

Mario Pei, *The Story of Language.* New York: Meridian Books, 1984. A classic study of language by the noted American linguist.

István Rácz, *Early Finnish Art: From Prehistory to the Middle Ages. New York:* Frederick A. Praeger, 1967. A collection of photographs illustrating ancient Finnish artifacts in chronological order from the end of the Ice Age to the Christian Era.

Fred Singleton, *A Short History of Finland.* Cambridge, England: Cambridge University Press, 1989. An easy-to-read history and analysis of Finland's development from the days of Swedish and Russian domination to the twentieth century. The author was a senior research fellow at the University of Bradford.

Eric Solsten and Sandra W. Meditz, eds., *Finland: A Country Study.* Washington, DC: Library of Congress, Federal Research Division, 1990. Basic information about Finland.

Rick Steves, *Scandinavia.* Emeryville, CA: Avalon Travel, 2002. A travel guide to Finland, Estonia, Sweden, Norway, and Denmark. There is only a small section on Finland, mostly Helsinki, but some interesting comments about Finland in relation to the other Nordic countries.

Deborah Swallow, *Culture Shock: A Guide to Customs and Etiquette: Finland.* Portland, OR: Graphic Arts Center, 2001. A very readable guide to Finland and the Finnish people written for business travelers.

PERIODICALS

Steve Blankinship, "Big Lessons for a Small Country," *Power Engineering,* April 2003.

"Finland Number One," *Earth Island Journal,* Autumn 2002.

Pirkko Pitkänen and Satu Kouki, "Meeting Foreign Cultures: A Survey of the Attitudes of Finnish Authorities Towards Immigrants and Immigration," *Journal of Ethnic and Migration Studies*, January 2002.

Wayne van Zwoll, "Finland's Finest," *Guns & Ammo*, June 2003.

INTERNET SOURCES

Joe Brady, "Finland Number One in 2003 World IT Report," Virtual Finland, February 2003. http://virtual.finland.fi.

Karen Christopher, "Family-Friendly Europe," *American Prospect*, April 8, 2002. www.prospect.org.

Eeva-Liisa Hallanaro, "Nature in Finland," Virtual Finland, September 2002. http://virtual.finland.fi.

Olavi Koivukangas, "European Immigration and Integration in Finland," Institute of Immigration, February 2003. www.utu.fi.

Jari Muikku, "Folk, Jazz, and Rock Music in Finland," Virtual Finland, 2000. http://virtual.finland.fi.

Aarne Reunala, "Forests and Finnish Culture," Virtual Finland, 2002. http://virtual.finland.fi.

WEB SITES

CIA World Factbook 2001 (www.cia.gov). Statistical information about Finland, including geography, demographics, economy, transportation, government, and military.

Finland Festivals (www.festivals.fi). Information about nearly seventy major festivals, organized by name, region, type, and date.

Finnfacts (www.finnfacts.com). Information on Finnish industry and the national economy. Includes a listing and description of more than fifty unique Finnish innovations.

Finnish Government (www.vn.fi). Information about Finland's government, including the president and prime minister, the council of ministers, and the parliament.

Helsingin Sanomat **International Edition** (www.helsinki-hs.net). Online version of Finland's major daily newspaper—

the *Helsinki News*—updated Monday through Friday, with many helpful links and archives.

National Research and Development Centre for Welfare and Health (www.stakes.fi). Affiliated with the Ministry of Social Affairs and Health to provide statistical information on social and health issues.

Statistics Finland (www.stat.fi). Up-to-date statistical information on Finland in several areas, from economy and health to environment and media.

Virtual Finland (http://virtual.finland.fi). An exceptional collection of hundreds of articles about Finland. Includes several categories, such as general information, history, environment, culture, education, and economy. Maintained by the press office of the Ministry for Foreign Affairs.

A Web History of Finland (http://ky.hkkk.fi). A comprehensive history of Finland maintained by amateur historian Pasi Kuoppamäki. Includes many illustrations and helpful links.

INDEX

Picture Credits

About the Author

Linda Hutchison lives in San Diego, California, and is a free-lance writer. She has a bachelor's degree in communications from California State University, Dominguez Hills.